COLLEGES IN THEIR COMMUNITIES

A dynamic nucleus

Margaret Sharp, NIACE and CFE

Published by the National Institute of Adult Continuing Education (England and Wales) on behalf of the Independent Commission on Colleges in their Communities

21 De Montfort Street
Leicester LE1 7GE
Company registration no. 2603322
Charity registration no. 1002775

© NIACE 2012

All rights reserved. No reproduction, copy or transmission of this publication may be made without the written permission of the publishers, save in accordance with the provisions of the Copyright, Designs and Patents Act 1988, or under the terms of any licence permitting limited copying issued by the Copyright Licensing Agency.

NIACE, the national organisation for adult learning, has a broad remit to promote lifelong learning opportunities for adults. NIACE works to develop increased participation in education and training, particularly for those who do not have easy access because of barriers of class, gender, age, race, language and culture, learning difficulties and disabilities, or insufficient financial resources.

You can find NIACE online at www.niace.org.uk

For more information on the Colleges in Their Communities Inquiry, a joint venture between NIACE, the Association of Colleges (AoC) and the 157 Group, and the original published documents, visit the Inquiry website at:
www.niace.org.uk/current-work/colleges-in-their-communities-inquiry

Cataloguing in Publication Data

A CIP record of this title is also available from the British Library

ISBN 978-1-86201-604-0

This report is also available as an e-book in the following formats:

PDF: 978-1-86201-606-7
ePub: 978-1-86201-606-4
Online: 978-1-86201-608-8
Kindle: 978-1-86201-607-1

For more information on NIACE's publications, visit: **http://shop.niace.org.uk**

Designed and typeset by Book Production Services, London
Printed by Page Bros, Norwich

CONTENTS

FOREWORD

The idea for a Commission of Inquiry into the role colleges play in their communities came from a meeting of NIACE's further education (FE) advisory group in early 2010. The group, which I chaired, had recently heard from Tom Schuller about the Inquiry into the Future for Lifelong Learning (IFLL). That Inquiry's report, *Learning Through Life*, had just become an adult education bestseller in the UK and further afield, mainly attributed to the depth of the research and the alternative, all-encompassing vision for lifelong learning it presented. We were also keen to hear more about the Inquiry's recommendation about colleges at the heart of a more locally accountable FE system. This vision would require colleges and government to change. But how?

With the formation of the first coalition government since before WWII, in May 2010, there seemed no better time to push forward with this agenda, given the need for innovative thinking and new ways of working. NIACE was keen to pursue this via a special Inquiry into this subject. Alan Tuckett, the CEO of NIACE at the time, had always been a strong advocate of the 'palaces of the people' - that colleges historically were the backbone of a lifelong learning system for adults. We agreed that the Inquiry should be a joint endeavour, with two college representative organisations I had close links with (AoC and 157 Group). All three organisations would nominate commissioners, and we were fortunate that Baroness Margaret Sharp agreed to keep us in order.

Margaret did more than that. Besides hosting us in the House of Lords, she added an politically realistic incisiveness to the debate, honed by years as an HE researcher. I learnt that inquiries are a good way of influencing public policy, providing the space to look at evidence over a period of time and test ideas while the policy context develops. At best, what results is a dialogue between the sector and government. In all this, our NIACE secretariat served us well. We were also lucky that senior officials were able to attend meetings as observers and contribute to debates and hear evidence.

Colleges in Their Communities: A Dynamic Nucleus outlines a process which I feel is not peculiar to the English or UK political context and almost merits a study in itself. It also speaks to colleges and providers of adult learning overseas. I have for many years been interested in models across the world, and have been fortunate to visit many community Colleges in the USA and institutions in Canada, Australia and The Gambia. The rooting of the Community College in its community always struck me as a very enabling mission. I was concerned that following incorporation and the increasing 'businessisation' of FE colleges that place at the heart of a community was being eroded. I was particularly keen to commission a literature review that allowed us to take into account the role of colleges and policy abroad. As our economies and the FE market become increasingly globalised, there is no better time to take a fresh look at things.

I retired as a college principal as the Inquiry was in its final stages, so it was interesting to see from a more distant perspective how effective the Inquiry was in generating a debate on the role of colleges at a crucial time. Since the report was published in November 2011 I have been impressed by how quickly government has adopted some of our central concerns and the central premise that we face a shared leadership challenge in industrialised countries wrestling with the need to invest in our nations' skills and well-being at a time when government has less resource. In my current roles as non-executive chair of a government body, researcher and writer, I see clearly that the challenge is for governors, employers, local leaders, as well as college staff, to work on this together. It is, as this report concludes, a shared agenda.

Sir Geoff Hall
May 2012

PART ONE
FULL REPORT

1 Introduction from the Chair of the Commission of Inquiry

This Commission was set up in January 2011 with the purpose of investigating the role that further education colleges can and do play within their communities, and the added public value that they can bring to those communities in their role as leaders of learning. Our remit required that the Inquiry was an independent one with its membership drawn from a wide range of stakeholders. In addition to the help and advice of colleagues on the Commission, I am grateful to the many people who responded to the calls for evidence, sent in case studies and invited me to visit their colleges. I would like in particular to thank Mark Ravenhall from NIACE who has guided me through this Inquiry and helped put this report together.

Further education colleges come from the twin traditions of working men's colleges and middle class philanthropy. Over the course of almost two centuries, individuals, employers, local communities and, more recently, central government have invested in, and benefited from, the delivery of this mix of liberal studies and family learning alongside vocational education and craft skills.

Today England's 347 colleges are present in almost every town and city, offering courses ranging from agriculture to the arts, helping some millions of young people and adults to gain and enhance their skills and education, providing pathways to better jobs and higher education. They are key players in the educational infrastructure of this country and, perhaps more importantly, a vital part of local employment and skills 'ecosystems'.

The communities they serve are diverse. They provide for young and old, public and private sector, employers and employees. The best colleges reach out to their communities and provide encouragement and leadership so that, in the words of the Prime Minister describing his Big Society vision, these communities are 'free and powerful enough to help themselves'.

Recent years have seen increasing government intervention in colleges. Almost twenty years of micro-management has led to a culture of following rather than taking the lead; of accepting, albeit grudgingly, instructions from above. The result is a funding and regulatory regime of immense complexity, which has consumed disproportionate top management time and resources. The aim of the Coalition government is to free up the system and give colleges greater discretion and flexibility to decide on their own priorities. Equally, budget restraints also require them to do so within a climate of 'more for less'. Our aim is to give some useful pointers as to how this might be achieved.

The report summarises the Commission's conclusions from the ten months of research, analysis and discussion and suggests a way forward. It is crucial we get this right. We believe colleges can not only help people into jobs through skills training, but, by being proactive in their work with local communities, can also harness the energy of those communities towards positive outcomes which in turn promote health, happiness and social cohesion. In doing so, the key is for colleges to work in partnership, whether with local business, charities, local authorities or public sector organisations. While colleges may be the catalyst for change – hence our term 'the dynamic nucleus' – we see the way forward as essentially 'a shared agenda'.

Margaret Sharp, Baroness Sharp of Guildford
House of Lords, November 2011

2 Executive summary

Our vision

The Commission's vision is of colleges as a 'dynamic nucleus' at the heart of their communities, promoting a shared agenda of activities which both fulfil their central role of providing learning and skills training to young people and adults, but also reach out into their communities, catalysing a whole range of further activities. We see the college as the central player in a network of partnerships, dynamic in the sense of developing and engaging with other partners. This enables the network itself to become part of the dynamic, with colleges at its heart.

The purpose of the inquiry

The Independent Commission on Colleges in Their Communities was set up in January 2011 to investigate the role that English further education colleges can and do play in their communities. Set within the context of a more flexible regulatory regime when colleges were once again asked to take responsibility for the shape and balance of educational offer to their locality. The Commission was tasked to report on the strategic role colleges can play and the added public value they can bring in leading learning and working within their communities.

The method

The Inquiry gathered evidence from a variety of sources. These were:

- A systematic review of national and international literature on further education.

- Two calls for evidence, the second following the publication of our interim report.
- Visits to colleges and discussion with staff and learners.
- Notes from discussions and presentations at commissioners' meetings.
- Thematic seminars for invited specialists and stakeholders.

The full evidence, including all papers, contributions and analysis, can be found on the Commission website: www.niace.org.uk /current -work/colleges-in-their-communities-inquiry.

Context

The further education sector in England is large and diverse. It includes general further education colleges, sixth-form colleges, land-based colleges, art, design and performing arts colleges and specialist-designated colleges, and serves a range of learners of different ages. Apart from the UK home nations, no other country's further education system mirrors the English system in terms of its diversity and reach.

With diversity, however, comes the awkward issue of public perception and reputation. It has been argued that colleges have a weak brand. Despite being the major provider of education and training for adults and young people, colleges have no clearly defined place in the learning and skills landscape. They do, however, often have very strong local brands, and are, in many cases, already active shapers in their communities, fostering aspiration and providing opportunities for individuals to advance their social, economic and personal ambitions.

Although colleges uniformly argue that their value lies precisely in their complexity and local reach, political interest in the sector has coalesced around reforms and initiatives to simplify their purpose. The Labour Government's post-Foster[1] view of the sector as,

---

1   Foster, A. (2005).

primarily, an engine for economic growth led to the marginalisation of the wider role colleges play in their communities and created a system of further education characterised by repeated top-down reform, ministerial target-setting and state micromanagement.

The current Coalition Government takes a wider view of the sector, and acknowledges its role in promoting inclusion and social mobility. It is seeking to introduce 'new freedoms and flexibilities' in the sector and to devolve greater responsibility for the system to local employers, learners and their communities. The proposed freedoms present challenges to funders and colleges to respond to the local skills agenda as well as to the demands of employers and individuals. However, funding is still constrained by rules and regulations as to what can be spent on which activity and, too often, college leaders spend more time managing 'upwards' to government than 'outwards' to their communities and beneficiaries.

Despite financial constraints and an overly complex funding system, many colleges are active in a wide range of partnerships, working closely with local authorities, the police and a wide range of agencies responsible for public health, social care, economic development and employment. More, however, needs to be done to help colleges play a leading role in local social and economic planning. In order to achieve long-lasting and effective social and economic impact on an area, there need to be collaborative approaches across the public sector.

Findings

We learned that further education colleges are, often, already embedded in their communities. Their provision is exceptionally diverse, with informal and non-accredited learning sitting alongside vocational and academic study. As well as providing learning and skills, many colleges have developed a significant wider role in their communities, contributing to widening access to learning, community cohesion and the development of civil society and enterprise.

Although there has been some simplification, colleges still have to negotiate an unduly complex funding regime. Confronted by cuts and other uncertainties on top of this already complex funding regime, some colleges opt to retreat to the low-risk areas of 16–19 provision and apprenticeships. Other colleges, however, have managed to negotiate their way through and have developed innovative programmes reaching out to marginalised, 'hard-to-reach' groups. These achievements have often been developed through creative partnerships.

Partnerships, while often rewarding, are expensive to negotiate. Negotiating partnership agreements, sometimes three- or four-way, takes a good deal of top management time, requires considerable resource input and carries further risks. Nevertheless, where successful, they unlock new resources, spread risk and can bring new, innovative ideas into play.

One lesson from abroad is the importance of local decision making, where 'local' means close to the consumer and the needs of the locality. Systems which give considerable autonomy to the local unit have tended to be more successful, as have governance regimes which recognise local stakeholder involvement.

In terms of meeting the skills needs of the local area, employer engagement is vital, but the most successful is engagement that goes beyond just treating employers as customers and involves them as co-designers of the skills training offer. Likewise, in terms of meeting the learner needs, the greater the involvement of learners in the design of the curriculum, the greater the buy-in, sense of ownership and achievement, the greater the success.

Colleges do not just make an impact on the local economy and the labour force needs of local businesses. In investing in colleges, we get social returns too.

Reaching out to disadvantaged, hard-to-reach groups within their communities not only leads to a steady supply of learners for higher-level, qualification-based study, but supports colleges' wider role in promoting the well-being and cohesion of their communities. This, in turn, leads to significant benefits in other areas of public policy, including health, social care, support for families, volunteering and the Big Society.

Conclusions

The best of our colleges are, in many respects, already fulfilling our vision of the college as a 'dynamic nucleus' at the heart of their communities. The aspiration is that all colleges should live up to the practice of the best. If this happens we feel it will help colleges to have a clearer role and develop a distinct brand, as their counterparts have in other countries.

The key is the formation of partnerships, which have the benefit both of spreading risks and of catalysing action. Through partnerships colleges can reach out to their communities and secure buy-in to their projects. Partnerships are essentially about establishing relationships of mutual trust which encourage all players to invest in the project, whether it is employers involved in a skills training initiative or a local authority in establishing a community hub in a deprived area.

Turning this vision into reality requires a new generation of entrepreneurial college leaders, and we recommend that the sector gives serious consideration to the establishment of a dedicated sector leadership centre which combines first-class training with guidance and peer support in building partnerships and taking and handling risk.

Colleges need to be working actively to develop partnerships with local employers to upgrade skills and create jobs. Many colleges already work closely with large employers in their area, but more needs to be done to reach out to small- and medium-sized enterprises (SMEs) using the new funding flexibilities.

Partnership with public-sector organisations is also essential to making joined-up government work at a local level. Colleges need to be proactive in seeking partnerships with local authorities, health providers, the police and youth offending teams, often in collaboration with charities and local community groups. Such partnerships yield substantial benefits, transforming the lives of individuals and the well-being of whole communities.

Colleges need to ensure that their voices are heard on local economic and social planning partnerships. Colleges are the main provider of skills training in many localities and they therefore need to be represented on Local Enterprise Partnerships, playing a prominent role in developing local skills strategies.

A new push into outreach activities requires new thinking about the curriculum. Providing routes and pathways to further learning is central but it needs also to be a highly flexible curriculum built to respond to local needs on an 'any time, any place' formula. Building confidence and self-esteem is important and so too is recognition of the motivational stimulus that people gain from group-based activities, whether in the college, the workplace or the community.

While the government has introduced new flexibilities, funding is still constrained by too many rules and regulations as to what is to be spent on which activity. If all colleges are to be innovative and entrepreneurial there needs to be a more flexible funding system giving colleges more discretion to be able to allocate resources as they see fit. An extension of the earned autonomy system might be appropriate. We also suggest that colleges, like universities, be subject to three-year rolling budgets.

Developing the community agenda for colleges requires a new approach to governance and accountability. The new Foundation Code of Governance for colleges sets out a new norm for community engagement. This might be developed to include guidance on ways in which colleges might engage with and account to their various communities on their performance to include good practice guidelines, benchmarks and performance indicators – something akin to a community compact.

Recommendations

In our interim report we referred to what we saw as a 'shared vision' for a renewed and revitalised further education system with colleges at its heart. Since then we have received a great deal of support for a shared agenda of reform involving colleges, their support bodies, and local and central government. We recommend the work be taken forward as follows:

Colleges to:

- Commence publication of college funding strategies that outline the levels of co-investment by state, employer, individual and other partners *(by September 2013)*.
- Define a clear offer from colleges to the communities they serve as specified within the proposed community compact *(by September 2012)*.
- Establish within colleges a clearly defined community curriculum that responds to local needs and associated educational outreach work *(by March 2013)*.
- Review HR strategies to reflect their community plans and introduce effective organisational support and development interventions and opportunities for all staff, leaders and governors *(by July 2012)*.
- Explore ways of helping local SMEs with apprenticeships and consultancy support *(by March 2013)*.

Local partnerships and commissioning bodies to:

- Ensure colleges are properly represented as joint partners in local employment and skills planning processes, building on the effective partnerships colleges have already established with bodies such as the Local Government Association and the British Chambers of Commerce *(by September 2012)*.
- Share existing public sector intelligence and data systems to increase common understanding of community needs *(by March 2012)*.
- Make sure that colleges are properly linked into the new commissioning bodies being established within the NHS *(by March 2013)*.

Central government agencies to:

- Establish an 'innovation code' to allow flexibility to fund responsive provision which meets locally assessed priority needs. This should total up to 25 per cent of the college's adult skills budget per annum *(by September 2012)*, rising to 50 per cent *(by September 2014)*.

- Establish a model and funding methodologies for three-year funding *(by September 2013)*.
- Review the Qualifications and Credit Framework to enable the development of flexible and responsive community qualifications *(during 2011/12)*.
- Define the self-regulation framework envisaged for colleges *(by summer 2012)*.
- Harmonise Ofsted (the official UK body for inspecting schools) inspection criteria on meeting community needs with those set out in the Foundation Code of Governance *(by April 2012)*.

Sector support bodies to:

- Develop a community curriculum template with tools to help institutions to develop an overall curriculum strategy and linked assessment system *(by September 2012)*.
- Establish a professional programme to develop a new responsive community curriculum via the Learning and Skills Improvement Service and the Institute for Learning *(by September 2012)*.
- Develop, through sector collaboration, good practice guidance and performance measures for community engagement *(by July 2012)*.
- Develop, with the Association of Colleges (AoC) Governors' Council, an annex to the Foundation Code of Governance that sets out norms for community engagement including supporting good practice guidance, benchmarks and performance indicators *(by July 2012)*.
- Identify funding to develop innovative and collaborative leadership programmes focused on the skills needed to address local issues and to create solutions *(by September 2012)*.
- Establish partnerships and programmes between the Institute for Learning and other professional networks to ensure synergy and effective professional development between staff and leaders *(by September 2012)*.
- Consider the formation of a dedicated college or sector leadership centre to ensure a strong focus on leadership and management for colleges *(by September 2012)*.

3 Our process and timetable

The Commission was set up in January 2011 to investigate the role that English further education colleges can and do play in their communities. This was set within the context of a more flexible regulatory regime when colleges were once again asked to take responsibility for the shape and balance of educational offer to their locality. The Commission was tasked to report on the strategic role colleges can play and the added public value they can bring in leading learning and working within their communities.

The remit of the Commission was to:

- review literature, existing national and international policies and models of delivery, and carry out necessary research;
- identify a vision, strategic framework and potential models of delivery for enhancing the role of colleges in their communities;
- identify 'practice worth sharing' on colleges in their communities and a strategy for sharing good practice; and
- make realistic recommendations to UK government and to the further education sector on the implementation of the proposed strategy.

The timetable for the Inquiry's work is summarised below.

December 2010	Appointment of Chair
January 2011	Appointment of Commissioners and Observers
February 2011	First meeting of the Commission
March 2011	Evidence collection: issue of Call for Evidence Literature Review phase 1 Second meeting of the Commission
April 2011	Evidence collection: Thematic seminars Literature Reviews for seminars

May 2011	Evidence collection: Thematic seminars (continued) Literature Review for seminars Review of evidence received from Call for Evidence
June 2011	Third meeting of the Commission Emerging findings and conclusions presented to the Commission Interim Report drafted
July 2011	Fourth meeting of the Commission Interim Report approved Further research and investigation
August 2011	Literature Review concluded Analysis of research and evidence concluded
September 2011	Fifth meeting of the Commission Findings, conclusions and recommendations presented to the Commission
October 2011	Sixth meeting of the Commission Final Report drafted
November 2011	Launch of Inquiry Report at AoC Conference

4 Our approach

The Inquiry gathered evidence from a variety of sources. These were:

- A systematic review of national and international literature on further education.
- Two calls for evidence, the second following the publication of our interim report.
- Visits to colleges and discussion with staff and learners.
- Notes from discussions and presentations at Commission meetings.
- Thematic seminars for invited specialists and stakeholders.

Colleges, stakeholders and other organisations with an interest in the Inquiry were invited to submit evidence to address the Inquiry's four research questions:

- What is the relationship between colleges and their communities?
- How do colleges contribute to local/community leadership?
- How do colleges develop, implement and refine national policies and plans?
- How do colleges define and arrive at a curriculum for their communities?

The Literature Review was carried out to identify, screen, categorise and analyse relevant published and unpublished literature. The process resulted in a detailed analysis of 289 documents, examining the nature of the relationship between colleges and their communities, and the ways in which the work of colleges impacts on learners, employers and their wider communities, along with issues of governance, leadership and accountability.

The expert seminar programme focused on six themes:

- Business and employer voice.
- Learner and citizen voice.

- Civil society and the wider community.
- Local social and economic planning.
- Curriculum and qualifications.
- Leadership and governance.

Each seminar was led by a Commissioner and had an invited audience drawn from colleges, learners, governors and stakeholder organisations. A total of 62 people participated, producing a rich source of evidence for the Inquiry. The interim report, published at the Inquiry's six-month mark, in July 2011, organised the findings under the six broad themes around which the six expert seminars had been convened.

A second call for evidence followed the publication of the interim report, adding to and further strengthening the case we set out there, and informing our final recommendations. We received over 100 responses to our two calls for evidence.

Details of the Inquiry's Commissioners and observers are given in Appendix 1. Appendix 2 provides details of all other contributors to the Inquiry's evidence-gathering process.

Documents summarising the evidence and case studies produced during the Inquiry are available from the Commission website at www.niace.org.uk/current-work/colleges-in-their-communities-inquiry

5 Context: colleges in their communities

Key strengths included extensive partnerships with local businesses, the local authority, schools and charities which create real projects that have high impact on both learners and the immediate community. These colleges are key players in the development of an effective community ethos. They develop strategies to engage hard-to-reach groups, and support them back into learning. Links with employers help them to become more competitive, enable them to secure their future workforce, and provide opportunities to local people. Students highly value work placements and have a very good choice of experiences through extensive links with employers, schools, nurseries, community organisations and universities.

Evidence to the Commission from Ofsted on college inspection reports, 2011[2]

What are further education colleges and what do they do?

The further education sector in England is large and diverse. It includes general further education colleges, sixth-form colleges, land-based colleges, art, design and performing arts colleges and specialist-designated colleges, and serves a range of learners of different ages. International comparisons suggest that, apart from the UK home nations, no other country's further education system mirrors the English system in terms of its diversity and reach. In 2009–10, English further education colleges educated and trained 3.4 million people. Eighty-six per cent of all students aged over 19 who received any sort of public funding in 2009–10 studied or trained at a Further Education (FE) college – 45 per cent (1.6 million) of the

---

2   Ofsted's full submission balanced key strengths with weaknesses. Not all colleges by any means lived up to these standards.

total further education student number. Ninety per cent of Skills for Life qualifications were achieved through FE institutions and more than 80 per cent of all ESOL (English for Speakers of Other Languages) learners were in colleges. As well as their adult and outreach activities, colleges make a vital community impact through their provision for 14–19-year-olds. In 2009–10, 831,000 16–18-year-olds were studying in colleges, compared with 423,000 in maintained schools, academies and city technology colleges. Forty-four per cent of those achieving a Level 3 qualification (A-level equivalent) by the age of 19 do so at a college, while colleges are responsible for a quarter of all apprenticeships delivered in England.

Further education colleges are autonomous institutions incorporated under statute and covered by the 1992 Further and Higher Education Act. They deliver a wide range of publicly funded and non-publicly funded provision to young people and adults on a full- and part-time basis, in a variety of formal and informal settings. Their activities are, in the main, funded and regulated by the Skills Funding Agency and the Young People's Learning Agency. Those that deliver higher education provision also receive direct funding from the Higher Education Funding Council for England. Further education colleges are led by a principal or chief executive with support from a senior management team and an independent board of governors. They develop their own strategic plans and associated objectives working within the regulatory framework set by the funding agencies on behalf of Government.

Further education colleges are primarily local institutions providing vocational, specialist and academic learning, as well as for community and personal development. Although they remain the most comprehensive component of the English education system, the range of learners studying in further education colleges has narrowed in recent years, with a pronounced shift towards younger learners. A slight majority of learners are currently under 19, but, until recently, as many as eight in ten were aged over 19.[3] Nevertheless, most adult learners still learn in or through colleges. There are colleges or college

---

3   NIACE (2005a).

campuses in practically every city and town, and rural areas. They vary in size: some are small specialist-designated colleges for adults, or subject-specialist colleges, but the majority by far are large, multi-site general further education colleges, some of which are bigger than universities in terms of student numbers.

In contrast to universities, however, further education colleges offer a highly diverse range of learning programmes and qualifications. Thousands of vocational qualifications sit alongside academic qualifications and a wide range of accredited and non-accredited adult programmes. Although colleges are minor providers of higher education – with 12 per cent of the market share – almost all of this is employer-facing. Half of all Foundation Degree students are taught in colleges, while colleges deliver 78 per cent of Higher National Certificates (HNCs) and 59 per cent of Higher National Diplomas (HNDs). Two-thirds of large employers who train their staff do so through college. Colleges are also responsible for 14 per cent of informal adult and community learning. It is generally acknowledged, by the government amongst others, that access to informal learning will help people to engage effectively in civil society and contribute more fully to their local community as well as to the economy.[4]

The weak perception of the college 'brand'

With diversity, however, comes the awkward issue of public perception and reputation. It has been argued that colleges have a weak brand (and that it is further weakened by the fact that any organisation can call itself a college). Despite being the major provider of education and training for adults and young people, colleges have no clearly defined place in the learning and skills landscape and are often overlooked in discussions of education policy. They have tended to be defined in terms of what they are not – that is, not a school or university –rather than in terms of their critical positive role in holding the system together and making it work.[5]

---

4   BIS (2010e).
5   See Schuller, T. and Watson, D. (2009), p. 4.

Colleges, however, often have a very strong *local* brand; 'local' in the sense of being known in their communities,[6] whether they be communities of place, interest or specialism. Many colleges are already engaged in the communities they serve, providing ongoing opportunities to individuals to develop their skills, knowledge and expertise and working with local employers to meet the specific needs of the local labour force. They have a critical role as a provider of learning for 60 per cent of our 16–19-year-olds and 80 per cent of adults. In these ways colleges are already shapers in their communities, fostering aspiration and providing opportunities for individuals to advance their social, economic and personal ambitions.

Colleges as an engine for economic growth

Although colleges uniformly argue that their value lies precisely in their complexity and local reach, political interest in the sector has coalesced around reforms and initiatives to simplify their purpose. Sir Andrew Foster's 2005 report, *Realising the potential: The future role of further education colleges*, called on colleges to develop a 'recognised brand' based on a 'shared core purpose' focused on improving employability and the supply of economically valuable skills. This emphasis, reinforced by Lord Leitch's 2006 report on skills, prompted a narrowing of the adult learning offer and a dramatic reduction in the number of adult learning places in further education. By 2008 adult learning was at its lowest level since Labour came to power in 1997.[7] The Labour Government's post-Foster view of the sector as primarily an engine for economic growth, combined with its acceptance of Leitch's over-simplification of the links between productivity and the acquisition of qualifications, marginalised the wider role colleges play in the lives of their communities.[8] Colleges were driven by targets based on qualifications, and success in turn

---

6   We decided to use the term 'communities' rather than 'community' in this inquiry. This is an important distinction: the plural is a helpful reminder of the plurality of communities both in terms of groups of people ('community groups'), but also of *types* of community (of interest, and today, of course, also virtual ones).

7   Aldridge, F. and Tuckett, A. (2009).

8   Leitch, S. (2006).

was measured by the achievement of qualifications. Professor Alison Wolf described it 'a bastion of Soviet style planning',[9] characterised by incessant top-down reform, ministerial target-setting and state micromanagement.

Devolved responsibility and community ownership

The current Coalition Government takes a wider view of the further education system and acknowledges its role in promoting inclusion and social mobility. It is seeking to devolve greater responsibility for the system to its users – local employers, learners and their communities. In his ministerial foreword to the 2011 further education consultation, *New Challenges, New Chances*, John Hayes, Minister of State for Further Education, Skills and Lifelong Learning, writes:

> *Learning and its consequences feed purposeful pride. It helps people feel a new sense of purpose and pride in the present and hope for the future.*

> *Opportunities for adults to gain new learning and skills throughout life are the portents of progress and the positive engagement of people with their communities. They are necessary for flexible, innovative and competitive businesses and the jobs they create. They are preconditions of personal growth and social mobility. They are guarantors of the values upon which our democracy is founded.*

> *Working together, colleges, training providers, employers, voluntary organisations and community groups can make an enormous contribution to restoring this country.*[10]

---

9 Wolf, A. (2009).
10 BIS (2010d).

The Coalition's vision for further education has emerged against a backdrop of rapid and uncharted public-sector reform, itself shaped by the global financial crisis and the need to reduce the national debt and stimulate growth. The dominant narrative of the Coalition's programme is localism: one of smaller government, a 'reinvigoration' of community leadership and action to support those areas where the state would have previously intervened. There is a strong belief across all areas of policy in putting 'power' and, sometimes, resources into the hands of service users to purchase the service they require and offering diversity of choice (i.e. competition between providers). At the same time, the Government has made a commitment to devolve trust to the professionals who deliver services, including school heads and the principals of colleges. The foreword to *Skills for Sustainable Growth*, the Coalition's skills strategy, states:

> *Freedom does not just mean abolishing stifling bureaucracy and meaningless targets. It means trusting people to do their job. The adult education movement was not born of Government, but of the people. And its primary accountability today should be not to the Government, but to the people it serves.*[11]

The Big Society agenda

The reforms are set within the context of the Coalition's Big Society agenda, which commits to 'give communities more powers' and to 'encourage people to take an active role in their communities'[12] to improve their own lives and the lives of those around them. These themes have implications both for the ways in which colleges respond as learning providers, and for the contribution that they make to their communities. This was recognised when colleges met with local government and the business community to share perspectives on how to promote local economic growth in a climate of severe funding constraint and to develop a common agenda.[13]

---

11 BIS (2010e).
12 Cabinet Office (2010).
13 Local Government Association/157 Group/British Chambers of Commerce (2010).

A paragraph from *Skills for Sustainable Growth*, under the heading 'Freedom', supports this:

Control should be devolved from central government to citizens, employers and communities so they can play a greater role in shaping services to ensure that they meet their needs efficiently. We will increase competition between training providers to encourage greater diversity of provision, including, for instance, FE colleges offering more Higher Education courses. This together with empowering learners by providing better information on quality and tackling poor performance will drive up standards. We will free providers from excessively bureaucratic control and centrally determined targets and radically simplify the formulae which determine funding for adult education, so that providers can effectively respond to the needs of business and learners.[14]

The Coalition's 'localism' and the Big Society ideas, with their emphasis on increased levels of community ownership and volunteering, have been well documented but not rigorously defined. In this regard they represent a huge opportunity for colleges and other providers to define what is meant by these terms locally and, therefore, how they are shaped and enacted. The Learning and Skills Improvement Service (LSIS) and the RSA, for example, have developed a new vision for further education 'that is fundamentally more collaborative, networked, and socially productive; where colleges are incubators of social value and hubs for service integration; where further education serves the needs of learners through being a creative partner in local growth and service reform agendas'.[15] This suggests that colleges should be shapers of reform as well as responding to it.

---

14 BIS (2010e).
15 RSA/LSIS (2011).

Funding reform and constraints

This principle of funding reform is reiterated by the Department for Business, Innovation and Skills (BIS)/Skills Funding Agency in the *Skills Investment Strategy*, published in parallel with the current skills strategy:

> *This Skills Investment Strategy sets out how we will reduce bureaucracy; remove unnecessary interference from intermediary agencies whether local, regional or national; streamline the organisational skills landscape; remove unnecessary regulation; and, introduce new freedoms and flexibilities. Collectively, these measures will ensure the sector is better able to meet the needs of individuals, businesses and local communities. ... Our objective is to deliver a skills system driven from the bottom up, able to respond to the needs of individuals, communities and an increasingly dynamic economy.*[16]

The proposed freedoms present challenges to funders and colleges alike to respond to the local skills agenda as well as to the demands of employers and individuals. For colleges, this freedom, if enacted, will mean greater control over what is offered, and how that 'offer' is developed and priced.

The situation is complicated by the influence of 14–19 policy from the Department for Education, which has the potential to distort the whole further education curriculum.[17] Colleges, already major players in the expansion of post-16 learning, now increasingly cater for students from 14 upwards, and the detailed implementation of the Wolf Report on vocational education, accepted in full by government, currently makes the 14–19 offer somewhat uncertain.

It ought also to be noted that, as the UK Commission for Employment and Skills has pointed out, Department for Work and Pensions (DWP) spending on employment and skills for unemployed adults represents almost half of the total spend on *adult skills*. Put

---

16 Skills Funding Agency (2010).
17 NIACE (2011).

together, the funding from the two departments now represents a significant resource in the system which could give colleges considerable leverage if there were really the discretion suggested by the skills strategies. However, this is far from the case, despite the recent successes with apprenticeships and the integration of employment and skills begun under the previous Labour Government.[18] Each department sticks to its own rules, sets its own targets and requires a separate set of accounts. This failure to develop joined-up government means a considerable fragmentation of effort.

Partnership working

Despite financial constraints colleges are involved in a wide range of partnerships working closely with local authorities, the police, and various agencies responsible for public health, social care, economic development and employment. A potentially important player to have emerged during the first year of the Coalition Government is the Local Enterprise Partnership (LEP).

LEPs are locally owned partnerships between local authorities and businesses, aimed at strengthening existing ways in which public funders, working with business and learning providers, can identify the employment and economic needs of their areas. They are seen by government as having 'a central role in determining local economic priorities and undertaking activities to drive economic growth and the creation of local jobs'. They are also expected to be 'a key vehicle in delivering government objectives for economic growth and decentralisation, whilst also providing a means for local authorities to work together with business in order to quicken the economic recovery'.[19]

---

18 UKCES (2011).
19 DCLG (2010a). www.communities.gov.uk/localgovernment/local/local enterprisepartnerships

Development has been slow, and the remit of LEPs is still beginning to emerge. Some LEPs are already pushing for a locally pooled skills budget.[20] However, it is still unclear how colleges will be involved and the lack of further education representation in the majority of LEPs is a serious concern. There are also wider worries about how representative these bodies are (by May 2011 only two LEPs were chaired by women and seven boards had no female appointments at all) and, therefore, how well placed they are to influence skills provision in a locality should their remit or ambition be extended. Colleges need to have a leading role here, helping local authorities to work with local employers, universities and other public and private sector institutions to develop a strategic overview of local skills needs and plans for how they might be met.

Leadership, accountability and collaboration

Leadership in colleges cannot be viewed in isolation from the wider context within which colleges operate, politically and financially. Colleges do their best to take a holistic approach to the issue of leadership and planning for the multiple communities and age groups they serve. But the separation of policy guidance and funding streams is a serious impediment to this process. The separate funding of 16–19 and adult learning, for example, is, for many, an artificial division. Nevertheless, the funding pressures, and the plethora of reforms and policy innovations they manage, mean that college leaders spend more time managing 'upwards' to government than 'outwards' to their communities and beneficiaries.

Colleges and communities often have different perceptions of accountability. For colleges accountability means audit procedures and representation on governing bodies as the main indicators of accountability; by contrast, communities may be more concerned with the practical manifestation of what colleges actually do in terms of delivering learning to their communities. This might include the

---

20 Bolton, T. (2011).

geographical location of learning centres, responsiveness to local issues, availability of transport, course fees or childcare facilities.

In order to achieve long-lasting and effective social and economic impact on an area, the need for collaborative approaches across the public sector seems so obvious. Pooling the local DWP employment spend, the Youth Offending Team expenditure on crime prevention and the college spend on skills training would avoid some duplication – there is a tendency for the same people to be recycled through the different programmes. This could provide extra resources, for example enabling those placed into jobs under DWP schemes to pursue further training and progression in employment. This, in turn, improves community incomes, reduces crime and generally adds to community health and well-being.

Squaring the economic with the community role

Our analysis of the current context within which English colleges operate can be presented as four quadrants. These are formed by two continua: one ranging from a predominately economic to a

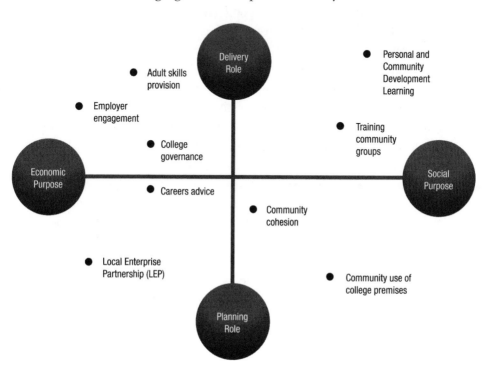

predominately social *purpose* for the college's activity; the other exemplifying a range of activity from a predominately planning to a predominately delivery *role* of skills provision.

This diagram exemplifies the vast range of activities that colleges engage in populating all four quadrants; the balance of college activity will depend on the local situation, the character and strength of its local partnerships, its local responsiveness and the way in which the college in question perceives its purpose.

The last decade of skills policy has encouraged a preponderance of activity in the northwest quadrant: delivery of learning for an economic purpose (through the achievement of full qualifications). This is the 'market for skills' that is being opened up to greater competition – a competitive environment that colleges by and large thrive in.

But colleges have the potential to do so much more than just deliver skills training for economic benefit. Many of their activities are for other purposes: skills maintenance; helping parents better support their children; helping new and settled communities learn English; helping people fulfil their ambitions. Some of this provision – especially that which comes closer to informal adult learning – has been increasingly difficult to fund over recent years. But many colleges have stuck with it because they know it brings substantial social returns.

Providers which occupy only the northwest quadrant in the diagram are those colleges with what might be called a 'narrow economic offering': they see their role as education and skills training and little else. Occupying the two western quadrants leads us to think about the planning role that the best colleges have and their contribution to more effective local, sub-regional and national decision-making. A college might occupy the two northern quadrants – this is a college that concentrates on teaching and learning but spends little time in developing partnerships. A college occupying all four quadrants might be called a 'rounded college', one that combines the economic and social purposes and builds an inclusive institution.

Colleges' unique position in the local skills 'ecosystem' means they have potential to respond to a wider range of social and economic issues than they have been asked to over recent years.

6 What we found

Many colleges are already embedded in their communities

Further education colleges occupy a pivotal space in the learning and skills landscape. Their provision is exceptionally diverse, with informal and non-accredited learning sitting alongside vocational and academic study. Their primary role is the provision of high-quality learning and skills serving both their immediate communities and broader 'interest' communities throughout the UK and abroad. At the same time many colleges have developed a significant wider role in their communities, contributing to widening access to learning, community cohesion and the development of civil society and enterprise.

Colleges have traditionally engaged with working-class communities through their vocational and adult education provision, and work with specific disadvantaged groups of adults and young people, often through partnership with the voluntary sector. This is also true of a number of other systems internationally, particularly the United States. The US's community college model has a decentralised system of governance and finance, with a remit to widen participation and encourage learners of all backgrounds and abilities. One notable success of this model is in improving access to higher education, which has been a primary focus of community colleges. However, almost 50 per cent of learners leave without a qualification, whereas the record of English colleges is much better.

The notion of the Big Society is underpinned by a belief that increased participation in learning can benefit wider communities by increasing education and skill levels which, in turn, will raise self-esteem, encouraging social and community cohesion. As major social entrepreneurs in their own right, colleges have a significant contribution to make, both in terms of encouraging adults to develop entrepreneurial skills and in coaching and supporting people in starting up and establishing new businesses. These approaches will only be effective if they are located in a context that is relevant to the individuals and their communities. Partnership with voluntary and community groups, already a feature of the work of many colleges, is necessary to develop an appropriate curriculum.

Barriers to entry to learning need to be understood from the learner's perspective: are individuals 'hard to reach' or are institutions 'hard to enter'? Outreach and development work are required to support the engagement of the most disadvantaged learners. Many move from basic and often non-accredited courses to the development of practical skills which support advocacy and democratic engagement. Involvement in such activities enhances the credibility and reputation of colleges and encourages more to pursue the path of learning. However, current funding regimes requiring, for example, co-investment from the learner even on basic skills courses such as ESOL are limiting the degree to which colleges can keep open these pathways.

But they still have to negotiate an unduly complex funding regime

Although in the last year there has been some simplification of the funding regime it still remains unduly prescriptive, with funding depending on such things as age, employment status and the level and aim of qualification sought. Confronted by cuts and other uncertainties on top of this already complex funding regime, some colleges opt to retreat to the low-risk areas of 16–19 provision and apprenticeships (even here, the funding regime discourages provision in communities where there is a risk of lower success rates). Other colleges, however, have been able to develop innovative programmes reaching out to marginalised, 'hard-to-reach' groups despite some of these constraints.

The curriculum offered by colleges cannot be considered in isolation from external strategic factors that drive or limit their abilities to respond. Funding and regulatory regimes are limiting factors in curriculum development and delivery, and the methodology relating to qualifications and units still effectively micromanages the way in which the budget stream can be used. This inevitably inhibits the flexibility of colleges' response to local and individual needs. Thus, the potential of the Qualifications and Credit Framework (QCF) to provide a flexible and accessible curriculum for adults is constrained by current funding methodologies. There is concern too that the perception of inspection and regulation systems can discourage innovation or work with non-traditional learners because of the potential impact on minimum performance levels, success rates and inspection grades. This may narrow rather than widen participation, particularly among the most disadvantaged adults. It may also discourage colleges from offering part or unit qualifications if success rates are still related to full qualifications.

Colleges which have succeeded in breaking free from the 'shackles' of the funding regime have often done so by developing a series of partnerships with other players, both public and private sector. Such partnerships have the advantage of both bringing in new resources and spreading risks amongst these players.

Colleges work in partnership with numerous different types of organisation to meet the skills needs of learners. Examples quoted in the Inquiry's Literature Review include: working with the Metropolitan Police to inform young people about the dangers of gang violence; working with local business, the local council and the DWP to provide unemployed people with specific skills; working with the local university and other further education colleges to develop a local hugher education hub; and working with schools and nursery centres to encourage parents to get involved with their children's education. There are also numerous examples of colleges working in partnership with local employers to develop and deliver training.

But partnerships, while often rewarding, are expensive to negotiate

Negotiating partnership agreements, sometimes involving multiple partners, takes a good deal of top management time, requires considerable resource input and carries further risks. Nevertheless, where successful, they unlock new resources, spread risk and can bring new, innovative ideas into play.

Recent research by the National Foundation for Educational Research (NFER)[21] which examined partnership work between colleges and local authorities highlighted a number of key lessons if collaboration was to be effective. These included: establishing relationships in which trust and openness were evident; having confidence that partners will deliver; sharing a vision and understanding of the project; regular and robust communication systems and the involvement of senior leadership. They also suggested that it was important to ensure that sufficient time and resources were dedicated to the partnership and that partners understood that other partners might operate in different ways and have competing priorities which would sometimes get in the way.

Nevertheless, partnership between different players at a local level can be immensely powerful and many colleges are playing a central role in creating such partnerships, despite financial constraint and the absence of a consistent approach to local skills planning. Already rooted in their communities in a variety of ways that add public value and contribute to social and economic well-being, colleges are centrally positioned between the educational community, on the one hand, and the employer community on the other. They work closely with local authorities and other local organisations, health organisations and the police. They also have links into community organisations such as youth groups and faith communities.

Partnership and collaboration are key elements in the implementation of our vision, with colleges acting as catalysts at the centre, forming partnerships with local employers, helping and supporting small and medium-sized enterprises (SMEs), and working closely with schools and universities, local authorities, voluntary and community groups, and other public services.

---

21 Reported in the Inquiry's Literature Review, see page 127.

The importance of local autonomy

Although international examples are of limited value in terms of direct transferability, one lesson from abroad is the importance of local decision making, where 'local' means close to the consumer and the needs of the locality. Systems which give considerable autonomy to the local unit have tended to be more successful, as have governance regimes which recognise local stakeholder involvement. Autonomy tends to encourage innovation and the development of new ideas. It can, however, lead to uneven standards unless there are also strong quality control and performance management systems.

The balance between the different communities served by a college is best achieved through local decision-making rather than by central direction. Local governance and accountability arrangements should inform these strategic planning decisions. The tensions between central policy direction and local accountability need to be addressed within the context of the public value that colleges bring to their communities. Colleges can demonstrate local leadership and responsiveness that illustrates the principles of localism in a practical way and yet sometimes be at variance with central policy direction.

Employer and learner engagement

Encouraged by successive governments, colleges have engaged with employers, small and large, either directly or indirectly, for some time, and take a wide range of approaches to the work. Some see their local business community as *customers* for learning products, others as *co-designers* of provision to meet specific business needs. The notion of a continuum ranging from selling to engagement through to co-design is a useful way of reflecting on colleges' relationship with employers and mirrors a similar continuum in relation to engagement and involvement of learners. All the evidence suggests that the more employers are engaged in the design and management of the learning process, the more satisfied they are.

Alignment between vocational education, the local labour market and the wider needs of the economy, has been a major theme of policy in most industrialised countries. A few systems – notably in Australia and Germany – include collaboration between government, industry and education providers in determining qualifications and curricula. Strong systems of apprenticeships are frequently a critical mechanism when it comes to ensuring employer engagement and investment, a particular issue in England where too few employers regard investment in training as a priority. In this regard it is important to engage employers more closely with Sector Skills Councils, whose responsibility it is to determine appropriate frameworks for different employment sectors.

The contribution colleges make to local skills delivery and their key place in the local economy means that they have a critical and under-exploited role in contributing to the development of local skills strategies. Their role should be better aligned with local social and economic planning, and in particular, with the emerging Local Enterprise Partnerships (LEPs). Colleges are often closer to local businesses than universities precisely because of their role as major skills providers in their areas. Working collaboratively with local business and local authorities on developing the local skills strategy can be a fruitful exercise for all involved.

There are particular problems in relation to SMEs. Their needs may be more diverse and less clearly articulated than those of larger businesses and finding time and people to develop links always poses a problem. They are a prime example of where outreach work may pay off, partly because they are likely to relate more readily to the college than to other organisations. It is often the learner in such cases who acts as the point of contact and mediates between the skills provider and employer – this happens frequently in apprenticeships. The Canadian example, where colleges offer consultancy and engineering services as well as skills training, suggests that the relationship could profitably be further developed.

There are considerable benefits to involving learners in the development of their own education. Research, reported in more detail in the Inquiry's Literature Review, has shown that taking account of learner voices can have positive outcomes for maintaining quality standards, improving the student learning experience[22] and the

---

22 Collinson, D. (2007).

learner motivation and engagement.[23] There is a wealth of good practice already undertaken by colleges in England and throughout the UK. There is also wide appreciation that a differentiated approach is required in capturing and responding to learner voices, with adult learners requiring a different approach to that employed for younger learners. Most colleges work along a continuum, with feedback from learners at one end and involvement in curriculum development at the other.

Providers that have gone furthest in embedding the learner voice into their practice have: instituted meetings between student representatives and the senior leadership team; introduced 'Principal's Question Time'; involved students in policy and strategy review; and implemented projects for students to rate their classrooms.[24] These mechanisms help to engage learners in the development of the curriculum and ensure that the learner voice is reflected in other aspects of organisation. They can be used to place learner voice at the heart of the learning experience while, at the same time, raising learners' expectations and encouraging learners to take more responsibility for their learning. The Inquiry found plenty of examples of colleges doing this and of the positive effect it can have on learners. The use of new digital technologies (for example SMS text messaging and online surveys to catch real-time feedback) has been found to be very effective with younger students.

The success of such initiatives depends on a number of factors, including the creation of trusting relationships between learners and educators, which, in turn, reflects the level of organisational buy-in to the concept of the learner voice.[25] In order to be effective the learner voice must be representative of all of the college's communities, both geographic and communities of interest. A strategic, whole-college approach is required to engage, understand and work with learner communities. College corporations need to develop a good understanding of what is relevant to learners from these different communities. Research suggests that although many

---

23 Forrest, C., Lawton, J., Adams, A., Louth, T. and Swain, I. (2007).
24 LSIS (2009b).
25 Shuttle, J. (2007).

of the more common practices are very effective at reaching full-time students, levels of engagement with those who are studying part-time or at a distance are poor. Colleges therefore need to put particular effort in to reaching into these communities.

In investing in colleges, we get social returns too

First and foremost, colleges are institutions of further education, established to deliver high-quality learning and skills to young people and adults. They have developed a range of methods of delivery in addition to their primarily campus-based, full-time offer designed to meet the wide-ranging learning needs of students and to widen participation. Colleges have implemented community-based initiatives to facilitate better access to those groups typically marginalised within a local area and have been successful in engaging disadvantaged and hard-to-reach learners, learners with low levels of literacy or numeracy skills, and adults with learning difficulties and disabilities. They also attract a culturally and ethnically diverse student body, with a higher representation of minority ethnic learners than the communities they serve.[26]

Reaching out to disadvantaged, hard-to-reach groups within their communities not only leads to a steady supply of learners for higher-level, qualification-based study, but supports colleges' wider role in promoting the well-being and cohesion of their communities. This, in turn, leads to significant benefits in other areas of public policy, including health, crime reduction, social care, support for families and volunteering.

Colleges are key strategic partners and their contribution and impact on society is often understated in relation to their economic role. This is not to deny that colleges are a significant part of their local economy. They are not only providers of learning but also major employers, and the owners and generators of community assets. But they are also major contributors to social welfare not least by the creation of learning communities and safe, tolerant spaces in which

---

26 Frumkin, L., Koutsoubou, M. and Vorausm, J. (2008).

people can come together to learn. This wider role of colleges is little understood but it can be crucial in, for example, metropolitan areas where gang culture exists. The college, as a neutral environment, provides a stress-free, safe haven for many young men and women.

The strategic contribution of colleges also should be recognised in the context of a shift to greater commissioning of public services where colleges could be involved in shaping and planning services relating to the areas they serve. A greater understanding of commissioning processes and commissioning cycles in the public sector, particularly in local authorities, would be beneficial. Experience from other public services, such as health, provides models where providers can both contribute to planning and engage in delivery without conflict of interest.

7 What we would like to see

Our vision is of colleges as a 'dynamic nucleus' at the heart of their communities, creating links and forging networks of partnerships – down into the education community, into the secondary and primary schools, the early years and Sure Start centres; and upwards towards small and large employers, local authorities, universities, hospitals, police, youth offending teams, youth services, community groups and housing associations.

We want to see colleges become prime players within their communities, promoting a shared agenda of activities which not only fulfils their central role of providing high-quality learning and skills training to young people and adults, but also reaches out into their communities, catalysing a whole range of further activities. These activities, in turn, bring more (potentially many more) people into the learning experience (and therefore, often, also into the college) and, in doing so, ignite an interest in participating and setting the agenda, whether in terms of the college itself or, more broadly, of their local communities.

There is nothing new in this: the best of our further education colleges are, in many respects, already fulfilling this vision, as active shapers within their communities, supporting social cohesion, creating aspiration and providing individuals with the wherewithal to advance their social, economic and personal ambitions. Our aspiration is that all colleges should live up to the practice of the best. If this happens we feel it will help colleges to have a clearer role and develop a distinct 'brand', as their counterparts have in other countries.

The key is the formation of partnerships. Partnerships bring with them the benefit both of spreading risk and of catalysing action. Through partnerships, colleges can reach out to their communities and secure wider buy-in to their projects. Partnerships are essentially about establishing relationships of mutual trust which encourage all players in the partnership to invest in the project, whether it is employers involved in a skills training initiative or a local authority involved in establishing a community hub in a deprived area.

We need to think about partnerships in new ways. They must mean more than simply 'more meetings'. Partnerships unlock social energy – people are often more willing to undertake activities, particularly where there are uncertainties, jointly rather than by themselves. For example, one college we encountered runs a community hub jointly with the local authority. This hub channels the energy of its young people into a boxing club and a cycling club, both of which now raise substantial sums for charity from sponsored activities. In other words, social energy channelled to positive ends increases both economic and social productivity. Improved levels of education and skills mean higher economic productivity. But the knock-on effects of self-confidence and self-esteem mean higher social productivity in terms of a lower incidence of crime, better health, happiness and community cohesion.

The college is seen, therefore, as the central player in a network of partnerships, dynamic in the sense of developing and engaging with other partners. This enables the network itself to become part of the dynamic, with the college at its heart.

Achieving our vision will not be easy. The right building blocks must be in place. In particular, in line with the ambitions of the Coalition Government's skills strategy, colleges must be given *greater funding freedoms and flexibilities*. In return, they will be expected to:

- Achieve higher levels of co-investment with employers, other public sector institutions and individuals.
- Play a greater role in local social and economic planning.
- Engage the local communities they serve in developing effective responses to community needs.
- Make greater use of their premises and other resources for wider community activities.

In order to achieve this, colleges will need to work with government on a *shared* agenda to:

- Revise governance and accountability mechanisms.
- Maximise cross-departmental co-operation and procedures.

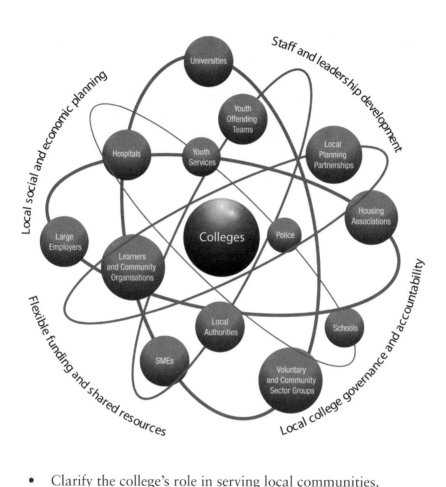

- Clarify the college's role in serving local communities.
- Remodel the college–community curriculum offer.
- Support staff, managers and leaders across all colleges to deliver this.

This is an ambitious agenda but we believe it is achievable because:

- There is the will and commitment from both government and colleges.
- All colleges are doing some aspects of this work already.
- There are many exemplars of good practices from the UK and overseas.
- Because of the success of these exemplars, there will be increasing pressure on *all* colleges to move in this direction.

Our recommendations set out in detail how we think we can achieve the vision. They are all, we believe, essential elements in creating a further education system that will give colleges the freedoms they need to innovate and experiment and respond flexibly to the needs of their communities, and balance this freedom with systems of governance which bring proper accountability but which, at the same time, reflect the wider public benefit to be gained from such activities.

8 How we think this can be achieved

Each of the following points represents an essential step in achieving the Commission's vision of colleges as a dynamic nucleus within their communities. We see each as a critical building block in creating a viable route for colleges to follow and envisage them being taken forward as part of a shared agenda of reform with colleges, sector support bodies, and local and central government.

A new generation of entrepreneurial college leaders

The most important factor required to turn this vision into reality is to support and train a new generation of college leaders who are both leaders and entrepreneurs. In order for colleges and government to meet each aspect of this shared agenda, the staff charged with responsibility for implementation and accountability, for ensuring their college is fully responsive to their communities, and for the outcomes articulated in this report, need appropriate, planned development and support.

College staff need to be skilled in securing routes of engagement with a wide range of local communities and in the co-creation of services, working across traditional organisational boundaries. They also need to possess the so-called 'softer' skills of empathy, emotional intelligence, working beyond formal authority and being able to take initiative and generate innovation, in real time, on the front line.

This requires a stronger focus on distributed leadership, professional autonomy and peer support and review. As well as developing and supporting the skills of teachers as specialists *and* educators *and* facilitators of new forms of learning opportunities. There is also a key role for support staff to ensure appropriate front-line customer services and back-office support. A new community-led pedagogy is also needed and we believe the key to making this happen is through fostering high-quality leadership with a clear and passionate focus on teaching and learning.

The Commission believes that a renewed and passionate focus by all staff and leaders on the importance of good-quality teaching and learning, and improved relationships with and responses to their local communities, are pivotal to success.

Approaches to staff and leadership development need also to acknowledge the changed and tighter fiscal context in which public services operate. The environment is one in which more is required with the same or fewer inputs. At the same time greater flexibility offers opportunities which can bring pay-offs but require taking risks. This is why we look to college leaders who are prepared to be entrepreneurs as well as leaders. It is also the reason training of college leaders should include risk taking and risk management.

> **The Working Men's College in London, UK employs Bangladeshi community outreach workers who successfully engage hard-to-reach ethnic minorities, particularly women reluctant to leave their homes, in learning English with other students. As a result of the work, students then engage in their local community and with their local schools. (The full case study is published on the Inquiry website.)**

Much leadership is innate, but it is vital to have a clear focus on leadership and the need for a balance and mix of college-led and sector-wide supported, designed and initiated interventions. Learning from ourselves, but also from others, outside colleges, was also highlighted. We recommend therefore that the sector should give serious consideration to the establishment of a dedicated college or sector leadership centre which combines first-class training with guidance and peer support in building partnerships and taking and handling risk.

Working Men's College, London, UK

As part of its commitment to encouraging community cohesion and ensuring that all its local communities have the English-language skills they need to get jobs, Working Men's College employed two Sylheti-speaking outreach workers to consult the large local Bangladeshi population, and involve them in planning how to meet their needs.

They worked with existing Bangladeshi organisations and other community groups, reaching groups of individuals with little or no experience of education. Two groups in particular were targeted: permanent residents, men and women, in the UK for over 20 years; and a group of younger women who arrived as wives and have been here for less than 10 years.

Working with local Bangladeshi groups and community centres, the outreach workers set up 22 English-language classes in places were learners were likely to feel comfortable and which had crèches (thus responding to one of the key barriers identified by these communities). They also established parents' classes in local schools.

As a result, the college gained a greater understanding of the needs of these communities, leading not only to the provision of English-language classes but also to courses in arts and crafts, childcare and IT. The outreach workers also set up an English class for Imams in response to the feeling expressed by some women that the Imams' poor understanding of language and culture was leading to conflict with young people.

Provision was qualification-bearing and supported by continuous advice and guidance in the core dialects. It took account of learners' final goals, which included finding a job; progressing to vocational or other courses; passing citizenship tests; talking to doctors and teachers; and acquiring employability or study skills.

As a result of their involvement, learners were found to make a greater contribution to their families and the local community, taking their children to museums, acting as translators, and getting voluntary or paid employment, including in local schools. Improved English skills also meant learners were able to meet and exchange learning and cultural experiences with other ethnic communities, through mixed classes and celebration events, thus promoting community cohesion in the area.

Working with local employers to upgrade skills and create jobs

High on the agenda in the present circumstances is the need to alleviate unemployment and create jobs. In this regard, colleges need to be working actively to develop partnerships with local employers, helping to fill skills gaps and working with them to tailor training to local needs. We believe colleges are more effective in meeting the needs of local business if they approach employer responsiveness as a shared agenda with a clear process of co-creating relevant services and programmes – rather than viewing employer involvement solely from a customer–provider or commissioner–subcontractor perspective. Colleges have engaged with employers for a long time but too frequently they treat employers as customers – buyers of their learning products – not as co-designers.

There is evidence of confusion regarding the role of business and disillusionment among some employers who feel their views are not being listened to or acted upon. Furthermore, despite the focus given to the creation of an employer-led system in policymaking, the evidence suggests that current mechanisms for engagement are focused on involving employers rather than on enlisting their support in the design of provision. As Ofsted told us, 'partnerships with employers are mostly good for vocational provision but opportunities for employers to support more generally are limited'. Too often, employers encounter a lack of clarity as to what is available locally and how this links to the labour market. They do not find it easy to find out who is responsible for local labour market planning, identifying skills gaps or taking action to address them.

Better governance and greater accountability are important here, as are leadership and management. It is critical that the key staff members responsible for meeting this new, shared agenda are responsive to the local business community, understand what is required in the new environment, and get the guidance and support they need. Colleges, employers and the wider community may have different perceptions of accountability, and new measures of accountability and approaches to governance may need to be developed to reflect local priorities and responsiveness.

Leicester College, Leicester, UK

Leicester College collaborated with developer Hammerson plc and the John Lewis Partnership to train unemployed people for jobs within Leicester's prestigious Highcross retail development. Hammerson was keen to recruit for the 2,000 jobs within the local community and, with its anchor tenant John Lewis, worked closely with the Retail Skills Centre at Leicester College, and in consultation with Skillsmart Retail, to develop a 'Retail Routeway to Work'.

Leicester City has high levels of unemployment, especially in some of its most disadvantaged and hard-to-reach communities. The Retail Routeway to Work offered unemployed locals the opportunity to take part in a two-week pre-employment training programme called 'Retail Works'.

The programme was written by Skillsmart Retail in consultation with national retailers including John Lewis, and covered topics such as customer service, selling skills and product knowledge. It was designed to provide retailers with 'retail ready' employees who matched their recruitment needs. It also provided job seekers with the knowledge, skills and confidence to apply for jobs within the retail sector.

All of the courses were managed and run by Leicester College. All tutors delivering Retail Works were ex-retail managers with extensive experience of the sector. Since the launch of Highcross Leicester, the Retail Skills Centre Leicester, now a member of the National Skills Academy for Retail, has continued to train those who are unemployed using the Retail Works programme as part of a Routeway to Work.

To date, it has successfully trained more than 1,200 individuals, around 60 per cent of whom have now gained employment within the retail sector locally. More than 600 of the new jobs created at Highcross were filled by previously unemployed people from local communities, with over 40 per cent of these new employees living in the city's most disadvantaged areas. The initiative won a National Training Award in 2010.

This is only one part of the solution. It is clear that colleges have a critically important role in supporting local employers in upgrading skills and creating jobs, as well in promoting and developing the entrepreneurial skills required to build the local economy. There are many examples of innovative business and community partnership work, from which we are keen to learn, and which deserve to be more widely shared, but good practice is frequently too dispersed with the lessons not being learned from one area to another.

Reaching out to smaller firms

Many colleges already work closely with large employers in their area, but more needs to be done by colleges to reach out to SMEs, using the new funding flexibilities. Colleges which engage with their local employers and SMEs often have a better understanding of local skills needs that wither local authorities or universities. There is considerable potential for colleges to work more closely with SMEs both in relation to apprenticeships but also through small-scale activities to support their business, with considerable benefits for both sides.

Here there are lessons to be learned from the Canadian model, where colleges work closely with SMEs not only to advise on skills requirements but to provide a range of hands-on advice and help services. A key strength of the Canadian system, in which community colleges are established by individual provinces, is the flexibility it affords colleges to respond to local need. Many colleges provide services or activities for the wider community, including supporting economic development; advising small businesses about industry practices; facilitating industry networks and collaboration; identifying business development opportunities for local employers; and targeting provision at specific industry needs to attract new business to an area. There is much we could learn from this hands-on approach to engaging business through facilitation activities.

South Thames College, London, UK

South Thames College has worked with employers to deliver an apprenticeship scheme that not only helps redress a major industry skills gap, but also offers learners long-term potential for a professional career in civil engineering.

The programme was set up with a consortium of six of the UK's largest engineering consultancies – Mott MacDonald, Arup, Capital Symonds, Halcrow, WSP and Hyder – to establish an advanced technician apprenticeship in civil engineering, a formal qualification for what is a skills gap in the industry.

The consortium approach meant that, between them, the employers could source a group of apprentices large enough for a training provider to be interested in putting on the programme. With the help of the National Apprenticeship Service, the consortium tendered for a training provider to deliver the programme and South Thames College won the bid.

One year in, and the Apprenticeship in Civil Engineering has proved a huge success. In December 2010 the consortium won the Mayor of London's Responsible Procurement Skills and Employment Award in recognition of the innovative and employer-led nature of the programme.

For the September 2011 intake the six original members of the consortium have been joined by a further five practices. Plans are also underway to replicate the consortium approach in other regions of the country, such as Leeds and Birmingham. In addition, the consortium is working with South Thames College and the Chartered Institute of Building Service Engineers to deliver a building services engineering technician programme alongside civil engineering.

Apprenticeship training has been immensely beneficial to the employers in both financial and social terms. In a period when all of the consortium members have seen major redundancy programmes amongst their staff (some as high as 20 per cent) all have continued to support the programmes and, as we move out of the recession, they are committed to increasing the number of technicians on the programme.

Apprentices also benefit from the training. They have an opportunity to work towards a well-respected professional qualification, with clear career pathways to chartered engineer status, whilst earning a living. And, working at some of the largest global engineering consultancies, they get to work on many of the world's iconic projects.

Niagara College, Ontario, Canada

Niagara College, in Ontario, Canada, utilises existing staff and students to conduct research with and on behalf of local industry. The college works in partnership with local businesses, small and large, to undertake research in areas of relevance and importance to the economic health of the region. Each semester 600 students are involved in course-based projects with more than 50 industry partners.

Niagara Research is part of Niagara College's Research and Innovation Division. Its main aims are to:

- support community and economic development in Niagara, Ontario and Canada;

- enhance the quality of academic programmes and the professional development of college personnel; and

- support the development of applied research skills of students.

It seeks to achieve these aims by:

- supporting economic development in the Niagara region and beyond through industry partnerships for appropriately applied research initiatives;

- conducting applied research and knowledge/technology transfer activities that help business, industry and the community develop and improve products, processes and services, solve problems and meet goals;

- encouraging opportunities for Niagara College staff and students to work with business, industry and the community to conduct research; and

- developing provincial and, where appropriate, national and international networks and alliances, with institutions with similar goals to advance research in the college setting.

The research activities are driven by the needs of the industries the college works with. The college acts as a hub for receiving research grants, conducting outreach activities to determine business/industry research and development needs or priorities, and managing intellectual property issues. It enables students to gain practical work experience whilst supporting industry to develop new products, evaluate services of develop strategies.

Colleges in the UK do, of course, already make significant contributions to the training and development of SMEs, which are often the main businesses in the localities served by colleges. They are, therefore, well placed to be a catalyst for the development of the small businesses sector through enterprise hubs that can train, encourage and support the growth of micro and small businesses.

Colleges are not just skills providers and planners; they are also a major part of the local economic infrastructure. They are large employers, and purchasers of goods and services. Their experience of working across the public–private sector interface means they are well-placed to advise other businesses on how to operate more efficiently and innovatively. We would like to see this role enhanced as colleges develop their community plans. In particular colleges need to explore new ways of helping local SMEs with apprenticeships and consultancy support.

Making joined-up government work at a local level

Partnership with public-sector organisations is also essential. Joined-up government may prove difficult at the national level, but it can be highly effective when put into practice at a local level. There are many good examples. We encountered numerous instances of colleges linking up with other public service providers, in areas such as youth justice, health and social care, parenting and family support, youth services and the police, to drive forward new partnerships aimed at promoting community well-being in one form or another.

Colleges, it should be remembered, do not just make an impact on the local economy and the labour force needs of local businesses; they make a major contribution to the health, well-being, culture, cohesion and reputation of a locality. This wider impact does not always get the attention given to colleges' economic role, but it is an area in which colleges make a real difference. Critically, the wider work colleges do in promoting the well-being and cohesion of their communities can lead to significant benefits in other areas of public policy, including health, social care, support for families, volunteering and the Big Society.

Unionlearn and Stephenson College, Leicestershire, UK

Unionlearn, the TUC's learning and skills organisation in the UK, has worked with a number of colleges in brokering protocols to promote learning and skills in the workplace. One example is Stephenson College in Leicestershire. Here, unions and local employers are working with the college to support the development of workplace learning and apprenticeships, as well as helping young people to enter the word of work.

Unionlearn and the college signed a protocol agreement which aimed to:

- support the development of workplace learning and skills in companies and organisations where there is union recognition;
- support the development of apprentices and other young people entering the world of work;
- provide information to students/apprentices on the role of trade unions and rights at work via briefings/resources; and
- promote activity on shared success stories.

As part of the protocol, unionlearn agreed to provide a strong and supportive framework for unions to maximise their members' future development by providing access to high-quality learning and by strengthening the union voice at work through the effective training of representatives and professional officers.

Stephenson College pioneered an 18-week programme to introduce young learners to brickwork, carpentry and joinery, painting and decorating, and plumbing, whilst improving their literacy, numeracy and IT skills. It also prepares students for the world of work by focusing on their personal and social development. By completing the course they are able to demonstrate that they are ready to take up an apprenticeship.

The college is working with unionlearn and local companies to provide the students with work experience and interview opportunities for apprentice employment. The course prepares students to apply for apprenticeships, where they will receive payment and on-the-job training. The protocol also ensures that students learn about the advantages of being a union member, including support with their future training needs.

Hull College, Hull, UK

As part of Hull College's wider community engagement, students from the college's construction department have been taking part in the Void Project, a joint venture, involving Hull Council, Probe, a not-for-profit community development organisation, and the Preston Road Development Trust, to transform four empty properties into decent homes.

The Hull College Group prides itself on listening and responding to the needs of its learners and also the local business community in which it operates. It is committed to ensuring that, when they leave the College, learners have the necessary skills and experience they need to succeed in the business world.

Hull College opened a site in the Preston Road area of the city to address construction skills shortages within the region, giving learners an opportunity to study for qualifications in the industry. The college has been working in partnership with industry organisations to develop an extensive collection of projects known as 'Pathways to Construction'. These projects are designed to maximise enterprise, business development and competitiveness in the industry.

The Preston Road Void Project gives construction students an opportunity to develop their skills by renovating four empty properties in the area, with a view to selling them on the open market as affordable properties. The first of these properties was completed in the summer and has been successfully sold. Further houses are to undergo their same refurbishment from this year.

Students working on their NVQ Level 2 course at Hull College have relished the chance to work on a construction site rather than in the college workshops. The challenge involves all aspects of property refurbishment, from 'stripping out' to joinery, plastering, bricklaying, fitting out and decorating.

Other recent developments at the college include partnership work to support advice and guidance for young people in the area, to help them make the right choices for their future; a project to give enterprising learners the tools they need to start their own businesses; and a dedicated business and enterprise centre in Harrogate, with the aim of enhancing the competitiveness of the region.

Ofsted told us weaker colleges have 'insufficient links with community partners and organisations to improve learning opportunities'. We know that such partnerships can yield substantial benefits, transforming the lives of individuals, the well-being of whole communities, as well as the quality of learning for existing college students. Colleges and their public-sector partners need to be bold, collaborative and entrepreneurial in making them happen.

Making the college voice heard on local planning partnerships

Colleges, as the major providers of skills training in many localities, have a key contribution to make to employment and skills planning as well as to delivery, and need to ensure that their voices are heard on local economic and social planning partnerships. They should have a prominent role in developing local skills strategies.

The Commission found that the competitive environment in which colleges and other providers operate sometimes hinders effective collaboration. Permissive approaches to partnership creation and loose alliances have led to a lack of consistency and role-clarity, and partnerships based on self-interest. Despite many years of heavy public investment, colleges are at risk of being under-utilised as a knowledge and physical resource in the communities they serve, though there are notable exceptions.

The economic impact of colleges is not only through the outcomes of skills delivery but also through their place in the local economy and their contribution to local decision-making. This deserves greater exploitation and alignment with new arrangements, such as the Local Enterprise Partnerships (LEPs) and, in particular, with local government's role in the economic growth agenda. This can lead to colleges working alongside employers, local authorities and other public services as strategic partners – often a fruitful relationship.

Plumpton College, Brighton, UK

Plumpton College, a land-based college to the north of Brighton, has taken an active role in hosting and supporting community activities. As well as providing 14–19, 19-plus, and extensive land-based education and training, the college has a conscious objective of providing support and other services to the communities it serve.

The college sees itself as a knowledge hub, conducting pure and applied research in land-based science, carrying out field trials and demonstrations of products and processes on behalf of land-based businesses, providing advisory services and farm management services, sometimes in return for other services or for wider relationship building, and hosting conferences on land-based and local economic issues.

It takes an active lead in hosting and supporting many other community activities. It has, for example, provided serviced accommodation and administrative support (particularly IT and telephone facilities) to a number of voluntary groups and rural charities, including the regional Farming and Wildlife Advisory Group, the East Sussex Proficiency Tests Council, the Sussex Young Farmers Club, and Farming and Countryside Education.

This saves these organisations the time and expense of finding premises and setting up shop on their own. Instead of rent, some of these bodies offer the college a portion of their staff time in support of college teaching or support operations. This provides the voluntary body with flexibility to take on full-time staff where their own needs may at least initially be only part-time.

The college infrastructure is available to the community throughout the year, on a 24/7 basis. Sussex police train their dogs on the college's estate; fire and rescue services practice recovering horses and cows that fall into ditches (training now offered by the college on a national basis); and Riding for the Disabled use its equine facilities, supported by staff and students. The college also organises and delivers weddings on the site, and rents out its sports hall and playing field and its residential accommodation during holidays. Its annual Open Day attracts between 10,000 and 15,000 visitors from across the county.

The college also encourages the involvement of students in the local community. They attend and provide demonstrations at county shows and local events, tend trees and gardens at local schools, and manage floral displays at Plumpton racecourse. College staff are also deeply involved in the community, often acting as trustees of many local voluntary groups and community forums.

Northern College, Yorkshire, UK

Northern College, in Yorkshire, is an active member of the Kirklees Adult Learning Partnership. The partnership, which is led by Kirklees Council, brings together local partners with an interest in adult learning to identify local needs and priorities for adult learning and to jointly plan provision. Working in partnership with Kirklees Council's Adult Learning Service, the college has provided training for community organisations to deliver learning and developed provision to encourage active citizenship and community cohesion.

The college has a longstanding relationship with a number of agencies in the Kirklees borough including the council's Adult Learning Service; Kirklees Neighbourhood Housing, an arm's length management organisation that manages the council's social housing stock; a number of neighbourhood-based tenants' and Residents' associations; and numerous third-sector organisations involved in community regeneration.

As a key member of the Kirklees Adult Learning Partnership, the college has worked with the council to support organisations to develop their capacity to deliver good-quality adult learning in the heart of some very deprived communities and worked with local learning champions to develop their skills as community advocates and leaders.

It has offered courses to Kirklees residents designed to encourage active citizenship and contribute to community cohesion. Courses have focused on topics such as: Getting Involved; Making a Difference; Introduction to Youth Work; Working With Parents; Issues in Mental Health; Young People and Crime; Introduction to Sustainable Living; Race, Ethnicity and Diversity; Recognising Issues of Substance Misuse; and Gangs and Guns.

The college has also supported learning providers to develop progression routes for adult learners and fostered the development of local partnership arrangements; and delivered Skills for Life qualifications to a wide range of community activists and volunteers and supported third sector organisations to develop their own Skills for Life strategies.

The work has been funded from a variety of sources, including mainstream Skills Funding Agency funding drawn down by the college; a joint bid with the Kirklees Adult Learning Service for LSIS Community Development Innovation funding; and the direct purchase of services by the agencies involved. One important factor in the success of the work has been the shared commitment of Northern College, Kirklees Council and a range of third-sector organisations to the goal of community empowerment and transformation. The partnership's shared aspiration is for communities to become more resilient and self-sufficient.

A vibrant learning and skills system is not concerned only with qualifications; it is about education in the wider sense. Further education colleges have an important role in the delivery of informal adult and community learning, working alongside local authorities, specialist-designated colleges and the voluntary sector to reach out to disadvantaged and hard-to-reach groups within the community. This work supports colleges' wider role in promoting the well-being and cohesion of their communities, leading also to substantial savings in, for example, health and welfare bills.

Developing a new curriculum

New initiatives towards outreach activities require new thinking about the curriculum. Providing routes and pathways to further learning is central, but it needs also to be a highly flexible curriculum built to respond to local needs on an 'any time, any place' formula and, for young people in particular, making full use of the internet and new social media. Building confidence and self-esteem is important and so too is recognition of the motivational stimulus that people gain from group-based activities, whether in the college, the workplace or the community. Hence, the need to blend online and distance learning with campus-based or even residential sessions.

Over the past decade the development and delivery of colleges' community curriculum offer has been limited by external strategic factors such as funding methodology restrictions and regulatory regimes which can discourage innovative accessible curriculum development aimed at non-traditional learners. Other limiting factors are qualification frameworks and awarding bodies programmes; and teacher training courses concentrating on the delivery and management of teaching at the expense of the philosophy behind curriculum design and development.

In spite of these constraints, the Coalition Government's reforms promise to enable a more flexible response to delivering services, learning opportunities and curriculum programmes. Increased investment in fees by individuals and employers, while challenging in a number of respects, also opens new doors and offers the potential for engaging a wider range of people.

Oxford and Cherwell Valley College, Oxford, UK

Oxford and Cherwell Valley College has, in partnership with Oxford Brookes University, developed a project which delivered a resident research and leadership programme in deprived areas of the local community. The programme was aimed at enabling residents to research learning needs and other issues and to empower them to respond.

In September 2009, the college broadened its partnership with Oxford Brookes University through the part-time secondment of its project manager for community development and programmes for the unemployed, to manage the university's European Challenge Initiative Fund project with the unemployed. By building on the community links already established by the college, this partnership project was able to significantly enhance the offer to the community by local education providers.

Two resident research and leadership courses were run in partnership with South Oxfordshire Housing Association (SOHA), one in Oxford and the other in Didcot; and two further courses were run in partnership with the Sunshine Children's Centre in Banbury. All the courses were based in the areas of highest deprivation in the county with the aim of encouraging local residents to become more active in their communities in terms of campaigning on local issues, mapping and finding out what local residents' needs were. The Oxford SOHA course targeted black and minority ethnic residents to take on a leadership role in the housing association.

Course content covered: exploring key ideas and concepts of what a community is and the needs of a community; an overview of community leadership and what makes an effective community leader; research methods for community development and leadership; and an exploration of some of the options and opportunities for leadership roles within the local community. The courses were run by tutors who were experienced in working with adults in the community or in research in the social sciences.

The courses at the Sunshine Children's Centre resulted in 80 per cent of the participants moving into work or onto further training and education. One learner won an award for his community enterprise proposal and one group engaged with Oxfordshire County Council in producing a walking map of the area. The impact on the SOHA black and minority ethnic group was also significant. One participant is now chair of SOHA's scrutiny group. Another set up a community website, runs IT courses across community venues, and has become a community tutor for both the college and the university. He was recently invited to a garden party at Buckingham Palace in recognition for his work in the community.

All the participants on the SOHA Didcot group were motivated to go on to do further courses ranging from maths and English to university degrees. One learner reported wanting to be 'a strong voice for residents', while another commented: 'I am surprised at what community entails. Now I know it is about geography, ethnicity, networks and identity/activity. I have acquired some knowledge of how to apply facts, combining them with skills and the right attitude to be able to influence policies and behaviour.'

Bishop Auckland College, County Durham, UK

Bishop Auckland College has, over the years, played a pivotal role in helping break down barriers to social inclusion for individuals and communities, largely through activities aimed at widening participation. In south and west Durham, the geographical area served by Bishop Auckland College, it has been, and is, at the heart of the communities through its network of community locations, including employers' premises, recruiting local people of all abilities and contributing to the social cohesion agenda of its catchment.

The college views its adult and community learning (ACL) provision as the access point to the college, providing learners with the confidence to learn and the desire to move on. The college recognises that ACL is intrinsically a partnership activity and the college has played a key role with a range of statutory, voluntary and community sector organisations, in developing the framework for ACL locally. This framework is concerned with developing skills for employment and lifelong learning which are important in achieving the aims of increasing social capital, smoothing social mobility, and realising social justice, enriching people's lives and bringing personal fulfilment.

To reach out to the communities across south and west Durham, the college has a dedicated Community Learning Team, based in community locations. The community learning ethos is to engage with individuals who would not necessarily feel equipped to take the step of participating in learning owing to a variety of social, economic and more specific barriers to learning. The college is also involved in the South and West Durham Learning and Skills Partnership, which is supported by localised partnerships of practitioners, sharing ideas and resources, jointly planning adult community learning provision and publishing and promoting the learning offer in each area.

The college and its partners recognise the importance of non-accredited learning and have developed a County Durham Learning (CDL) quality framework aimed at ensuring that learners have definite aims, structure and quality assurance in their learning experiences. The framework sets out how quality assurance can be achieved for non-accredited learning, providing a check list of good practice that will help organisations to meet the requirements of various funding bodies and Inspectorate.

A new 'community curriculum' would reflect the commitment to providing local responsiveness. The key features of curriculum design would be to:

- *Communicate with a college's communities in a manner which they understand and with which they can engage.*
- *Develop aspects of learning in a way, and at a time and place, which will involve the majority of the targeted group.* A curriculum needs to include an assessment methodology both formative and summative which moves learning forward and does not merely judge what has been learned. It must add to the process of learning, building upon existing skills and capabilities and further developing an individual.
- *Reflect the distinction between younger people's learning and the often more episodic way in which adults learn.* It should recognise the different starting points and learning experiences of younger learners whose brain functions are different from those of older, more analogue adult learners who will not have experienced the same level of technology or the national curriculum.

The design of a community curriculum should:

- Reflect the different learning experiences of adults and develop confidence and self-esteem.
- Be delivered locally and responsively, comprising a series of short or part-time learning experiences rather than merely longer-term linear courses.
- Provide different routes and pathways to learning in a flexible way.
- Ensure that the process of learning and appropriateness of assessment and feedback methods are critical and of equal importance to the content.
- Offer highly flexible, any-time, any-place provision, and support episodic learning.
- Build upon the wide range of experiences and skills adults bring to learning.
- Encourage enterprise and the development of business start-up skills within vocational areas of learning.

- Encourage adults to get involved in the life of the college through mentoring and coaching, employment opportunities and the learning voice.
- Be supported by professional development to enable the assessment of community needs, the development of curriculum philosophy and design and the implementation of curriculum and assessment methodology.

A more flexible funding system

The world-class further and higher education system we enjoy today is the result of years of investment from the public purse. Whatever the future status of colleges in the public, private or third sectors, they are assets in which we have all invested and from which communities have a right to benefit. Their common denominator is that they are currently not-for-profit bodies where any surplus is ploughed back into the business. In challenging economic times it is important to allow these social businesses as much space as possible to flourish and play a full part in their local economies.

While the Coalition Government deserves credit for introducing considerably more flexibilities than under the previous system, funding is still constrained by too many rules and regulations as to what is to be spent on which activity. If all colleges are to be innovative and entrepreneurial they need more discretion to be able to allocate resources as they see fit.

There are two main causes of concern expressed by colleges:

- An insecure funding base that hinders innovation and development.
- Micromanagement of funding detail by government agencies that discourages cross-subsidy and direct college response/discretion to local and individual needs.

The achievement of the vision of this report hinges on the ability of colleges to respond flexibly and responsively to their very different local economies and communities.

City College Norwich, Norwich, UK

For the last two years students from the college have worked with Norwich Day Services to improve the environment for service-users by undertaking a complete garden makeover at one of their day centres. The two-stage project has benefitted adults with learning difficulties and those with dementia who use the centre.

In each stage, the project has brought together students from across the college to put their skills into practice for the community. The work has also seen the students working directly with the service-users in planning the makeover of the gardens at Norwich Day Services' Harford Hill Centre on Ipswich Road.

During the first phase of work, students on the Young Apprenticeship in Construction created three raised beds and a paved area, putting in time during their half-term holiday to complete the work. Two groups on the Diploma in Society, Health and Development then planted the new garden area with a variety of spring flowering plants and shrubs, salad plants and other summer flowering plants grown by Progressions Horticulture students from the college's School of Foundation Studies.

The second stage was completed earlier this year. Foundation Degree Arts and Wellbeing student Anne Goodhew helped design the adjoining garden area. Prince's Trust students laid a new paved area. Construction and the Built Environment students designed and built a gazebo, and Health and Social Care students, together with Foundation Flexi Horticulture and Foundation Access students, filled troughs and hanging baskets. Creative and Media students also got involved, creating a sixties inspired mural, whilst Health and Social Care students created sensory items for the garden.

All of the students benefitted immensely from their participation, gaining added motivation and satisfaction from the knowledge that they were using their skills to help others. Society, Health and Development Diploma student Sam Meeks summed up the feeling, when she said, 'It was hard work... [but] we got a real sense of achievement out of it'.

There were also benefits for the day centre service users' from working with the students. Centre manager Chris Bishop commented: 'The people who use our service gain a lot from the interactions they have with the work placement students from City College Norwich. We have seen an increase in their confidence and social skills as a result of working alongside the students as equal partners on this project.'

City College Norwich has a well-established partnership with Norwich Day Services, which regularly provides work placements to the College's Health and Social Care students, a number of whom have subsequently gone on to work for the organisation. The college was able to use its relationships with local employers to support the project, securing building materials and other garden supplies free of charge or at greatly discounted rates for the project.

In our interim report we argued for a number of immediate and longer-term changes to the funding regime. In particular, we asked government to allow colleges to:

- Use up to 25 per cent of their adult skills budget to meet locally assessed priority needs.
- Pilot the funding of outcomes as opposed to student numbers or qualification outputs.
- Pilot three-year funding for outstanding colleges.
- Review and amend the funding guidance and audit regime, stripping out the detailed bureaucratic controls.

These ideas have received broad support and the Coalition Government's reform programme has continued to take a direction of travel that moves the sector towards the shared agenda we outlined in July 2011.

A new approach to governance and accountability

The shift in public policy from centrally planned systems towards greater local discretion and responsibility means greater autonomy for colleges, and a continuing streamlining of top-down regulation and direction, particularly for those colleges demonstrating good results and sound finances. It also means placing a greater emphasis on accountability to the people colleges serve, rather than to government or its agencies. Developing the community agenda for colleges requires new thinking about governance and accountability.

A college's accountability to its communities is different in nature from its traditional accountability to central regulators and funders. Community bodies will not have regulatory oversight of what a college delivers, nor will they have commissioning powers (except where they are co-funding provision). A college's duty is to engage with its communities in order to develop a common view on priority skills needs and how they can best be met; and to explain and discuss its performance in meeting them. We see responsibility for balancing the competing priorities of different users as lying with the college.

The governing body of a college is key to this process. It sets strategic priorities in the light of both the policies of government and funding agencies, and the training needs identified by communities. However, governing bodies sometimes experience tension between their engagement with communities and their statutory responsibilities in relation to quality and financial performance. In both these areas, colleges are subject to prescriptive top-down supervision and regulation by Ofsted and the Skills Funding Agency respectively. Many feel that upward accountability to regulators has stunted the development of processes for answering to the communities they serve.

We have considered a number of approaches to dealing with these tensions, and ensuring that governing bodies deepen their engagement with communities to get a better understanding of local needs and priorities, and to explain performance and future plans in helping to meet them. To be durable, the approach needs to go with the grain of the Coalition Government's plans to reduce prescriptive external regulation and move towards greater self-regulation. The government plans to give colleges freedom to streamline their Instruments and Articles of Governance, while retaining some core duties on governing bodies. We welcome this, but believe that the duties should be extended in two ways. First, in preparing their business plans corporations should have regard to the skills needs of the communities they serve. This would help embed a community focus more universally across the college sector, and require governors to balance the needs of their communities against their other duties in respect of quality and financial performance. Second, corporations should be given a new statutory duty in their Articles to account, probably annually, to their various communities on their performance in meeting local needs. This is required in order to provide the basis for regular open dialogue.

Along with this new autonomy, it is important for colleges to become a good deal more transparent about their performance and future plans for meeting their communities' skills needs. The new Foundation Code of Governance for colleges, due to come into force next year, already sets out a new norm for community engagement. This might be developed to include guidance on ways in which colleges might engage with and account to their various communities on their performance to include good practice guidelines, benchmarks and performance indicators. One possibility is to extend this section of the Code into an fully fledged 'compact' negotiated with the local community and setting out explicitly and with greater transparency the college's community offer and expected outcomes against which progress might be measured.

York College, York, UK

York College governors use their links with community organisations well and the college restructured its governing body committees in 2008 to facilitate a better understanding of skills needed in the local area. It then reviewed and further restructured its employer and skills committee in 2010, expanding the membership and remit to make sure it kept up to date with the needs of businesses and skills in the local community.

The committee is chaired by a governor who is Director of City Strategy and Deputy Chief Executive of the City of York Council. This provides the college with a direct link to the city's economic and social policies. The committee's members include key local and regional employers, providing them with opportunity to influence the college's strategic direction in this area of work.

The committee hosts an annual consultation activity with a full range of local employers, and ensures the college's strategy is based upon feedback gathered at that event. During the year, the committee members also oversee the college's employer-engagement activities, advise on marketing and engagement with businesses, and monitor and direct improvement work as well as acting as advisers and advocates for the college more generally.

In addition to this work, the full governing body is regularly briefed by the Principal and other senior managers on the way the college gathers information on community needs and responds to these through its operational and strategic planning activities. The college operates in line with a set of values which includes the statement: 'As a way of fostering learning, York College values working together to meet the needs of our College and the wider community.'

9 A shared agenda

In our interim report we argued that if government would respond to our suggestion for a loosening of the over-rigorous funding regime and a lessening of bureaucracy then colleges would, for their part, deliver in terms of community leadership, closer engagement with employers and learners and acceptance of greater local accountability.

Since then we have received a great deal of support for this shared agenda of reform with colleges, their support bodies, and local and central government all being prepared to play their part. The planning and implementation of the precise details of how this will be taken forward will be a product of collaboration between these agencies – we are delighted that work has already stated in this regard.

Colleges to:

- Commence publication of college funding strategies that outline the levels of co-investment by state, employer, individual and other partners *(by September 2013)*.
- Define a clear offer from colleges to the communities they serve as specified within the proposed community compact *(by September 2012)*.
- Establish within colleges a clearly defined community curriculum that responds to local needs and associated educational outreach work *(by March 2013)*.
- Review HR strategies to reflect their community plans and introduce effective organisational support and development interventions and opportunities for all staff, leaders and governors *(by July 2012)*.
- Explore ways of helping local SMEs with apprenticeships and consultancy support *(by March 2013)*.

Local partnerships and commissioning bodies to:

- Ensure colleges are properly represented as joint partners in local employment and skills planning processes, building on the effective partnerships colleges have already established with bodies such as the Local Government Association and the British Chambers of Commerce *(by September 2012)*.
- Share existing public sector intelligence and data systems to increase common understanding of community needs *(by March 2012)*.
- Make sure that colleges are properly linked into the new commissioning bodies being established within the NHS *(by March 2013)*.

Central government agencies to:

- Establish an 'innovation code' to allow flexibility to fund responsive provision which meets locally assessed priority needs. This should total up to 25 per cent of the college's adult skills budget per annum *(by September 2012)*, rising to 50 per cent *(by September 2014)*.
- Establish a model and funding methodologies for three-year funding *(by September 2013)*.
- Review the Qualifications and Credit Framework to enable the development of flexible and responsive community qualifications *(during 2011/12)*.
- Define the self-regulation framework envisaged for colleges *(by summer 2012)*.
- Harmonise Ofsted inspection criteria on meeting community needs with those set out in the Foundation Code of Governance *(by April 2012)*.

Sector support bodies to:

- Develop a community curriculum template with tools to help institutions to develop an overall curriculum strategy and linked assessment system *(by September 2012)*.
- Establish a professional programme to develop a new responsive community curriculum via the Learning and Skills Improvement Service and the Institute for Learning *(by September 2012)*.
- Develop, through sector collaboration, good practice guidance and performance measures for community engagement *(by July 2012)*.
- Develop, with the AoC Governors' Council, an annex to the Foundation Code of Governance that sets out norms for community engagement including supporting good practice guidance, benchmarks and performance indicators *(by July 2012)*.
- Identify funding to develop innovative and collaborative leadership programmes focused on the skills needed to address local issues and to create solutions *(by September 2012)*.
- Establish partnerships and programmes between the Institute for Learning and other professional networks to ensure synergy and effective professional development between staff and leaders *(by September 2012)*.
- Consider the formation of a dedicated college or sector leadership centre to ensure a strong focus on leadership and management for colleges *(by September 2012)*.

Appendix 1: Contributors to the Inquiry

Commissioners

Margaret Sharp, Baroness Sharp of Guildford – Chair of the Inquiry
Mike Atkinson – Governor, Plumpton College
Denise Brown-Sackey – Principal, Newham College (from May 2011)
Michelle Dawson – Community Manager, Hammerson PLC
Sally Dicketts – Principal, Oxford and Cherwell Valley College
Beverley Evans – Chair, Local Education Authorities Forum for the
    Education of Adults (LEAFEA)
Maggie Galliers CBE – Principal, Leicester College
Satnam Gill OBE – Principal, Working Men's College, Camden
Geoff Hall – Principal, New College Nottingham (until May 2011)
Stella Mbubaegbu CBE – Principal and Chief Executive, Highbury
    College
Elaine McMahon CBE – Chief Executive and Principal, Hull College
David McNulty – Chief Executive, Surrey County Council
Chris Morecroft – President, Association of Colleges (AoC)
Lynne Sedgmore CBE – Executive Director, 157 Group
John Widdowson CBE – Principal and Chief Executive, New College
    Durham
Tom Wilson – Director, unionlearn

Observers

Verity Bullough – Executive Director, Capacity and Infrastructure,
    Skills Funding Agency (from June 2011)
Lorna Fitzjohn – Divisional Manager, Learning and Skills, Ofsted
David Hughes – National Director of College and Learning Provider
    Services, Skills Funding Agency (until May 2011; from September
    2011 as Chief Executive, NIACE)

Bobbie McClelland – Deputy Director for Post-19 Landscape, Department for Business, Innovation and Skills (BIS)

Alison Morris – Senior Manager, UK Commission for Employment and Skills

Alan Tuckett OBE – Chief Executive, NIACE (until August 2011)

Rob Wye – Chief Executive, Learning and Skills Improvement Service

Project Team

Mark Ravenhall – Director of Policy and Impact, NIACE

Joy Mercer – Director of Policy (Education), AoC

Ian Yarroll – Programme Manager, NIACE

Dr Fiona Aldridge – Research Manager, NIACE (until June 2011)

Lindsey Bowes – Senior Research Manager, CFE

Amy Goodall – Project Administrator, NIACE

Emily Jones, Research Assistant, NIACE

Sarah Neat – Senior Research Executive, CFE

Dr Helen Plant – Research Manager, NIACE (from June 2011)

Dr Paul Stanistreet – Editor, *Adults Learning*

Appendix 2: Acknowledgements

NIACE would like to thank the Department for Business, Innovation and Skills, and the Skills Funding Agency for their support for part of the research and development programme that led to this report.

Thanks to:

The Inquiry's research partner CFE for their work on their comprehensive Literature Review, and Dr Jan Eldred for her peer review of the literature.

Those colleagues (in addition to those named above) who contributed their expertise to the seminar series and Commission meetings:

Mercy Addo, Department for Business, Innovation and Skills (BIS)
Titus Alexander, Democracy Matters
Liz Armstrong, Oxford and Cherwell Valley College
Mike Bell, Skills Funding Agency
Richard Bolsin, Workers' Educational Association (WEA)
Joanna Cain, UNISON
Bert Clough, TUC unionlearn
Sandy Connors, South Essex College
Mike Davis, Ofsted
Abigail Diamond, CFE
John Everard, Northern College
John Gamble, Skills Funding Agency
Marina Gaze, Ofsted
Keith Gilson, Houlton
David Golding, Stockport College
Denise Hayhurst, Blackburn College
Paul Head, The College of Haringey, Enfield and North East London
Anthony Hemmings, Burton and South Derbyshire College
John Holmes, Urban Matters
Karen Ingram, BIS

Kathryn James, LSIS
Leon Jenkins, North West Kent College
Suzanna Johnson, Mary Ward Centre
Beverley Jones, North Hertfordshire College
Robin Jones, Waltham Forest College
Tracey Kinsley, Leicester College
Gemma Knott, 157 Group
Abi Lammas, LSIS
Peter Lavender, NIACE
Liz Leek, New College Nottingham
Janice Logie, Essex County Council
Holly Manley, Apprentice of the Year 2010
Chris Minter, Leicester City Council
Judith Mobbs, Suffolk County Council
Frank Offer, Surrey County Council
Alice Pethic, Warwickshire College
David Pine, Sussex Coast College
Lee Probert, Hull College Group
Hilary Rimmer, Birmingham Metropolitan College
Steven Roberts, Cornwall College
Mark Robertson, South Staffordshire College
Irina Stanera, Working Men's College, Camden
Steve Stanley, Ofsted
David Steadman, Falmouth Marine School
Richard Stevens, Hull City Council
Helen Stevenson, Derby College
Selina Stewart, Joseph Chamberlain College
Dan Taubman, UCU
Cathy Taylor, Sirius Academy
Ann Walker, WEA
Gary Warke, Hull College
Andy Wilson, Westminster Kingsway College
Tony Woodward, Strode's College

Staff, students and stakeholders at the following colleges visited by the chair:

Barnsley College
Bolton Community College
Bradford College
City Literary Institute, Holborn
Hull College
Leicester College
Newham College of Further Education
North Warwickshire and Hinckley College
Northern College
Oldham Sixth Form College Science Centre
South Thames College
Working Men's College, Camden

Further submissions of evidence

Denis Allison, Trustee of Horden Youth and Community Centre
Ruth Auton
Tony Bartley, Sandbach School
Bassingbourn Village College
David Bell, Asset Skills
Shane Chowen, Institute for Learning
Teresa Cole, Head of Community College, Highbury College
Professor David Collinson, Lancaster University
June Davison, Northumbria University
Derby City Council Adult Learning Service
Devon Community Learning Partnership
Colin Farmery, St Vincent College
Sandie Foster, Royal National College for the Blind
Julie Hinchliffe, Bradford College
Jeremy Holloway
Azara Issifu, BIMATA Associates
Professor David James, Bristol Centre for Research in Lifelong Learning and Education
Gemma Knott, 157 Group

The Lancashire Colleges
Lancaster and Morecambe College
Macclesfield College
Manchester City Council
The Manchester College
Manchester Third Sector Learning, Skills and Employment Network
Iain McKinnon
Andrew Morris
David Nelson
Tra My Nguyen, Ofsted
North West Local Education Authority Forum for the Education of
    Adults
Judith Pelham, learner
Jayne Quantrill, Forward Communities
Sue Somerville, Bolton Council
South Devon College
Sussex Coast College Hastings
Jill Taylor, KTS Training

Case studies provided by:

Bishop Auckland College
Hull College
Leicester College/Hammersons plc
Northern College
Norwich City College
Oxford and Cherwell Valley College
Plumpton College
South Thames College
unionlearn/Stephenson College
Working Men's College, Camden
York College

PART TWO

FINAL LITERATURE REVIEW

Contributed by CFE, www.cfe.org.uk

Abstract

This systematic review of national and international literature on Further Education was produced for the Inquiry into Colleges in Their Communities chaired by Baroness Sharp of Guilford. The Inquiry was set up in January 2011 to investigate the role of, and public value added by, Further Education Colleges in England. The literature review explores the nature of the relationship between colleges and their communities in order to establish how they identify and meet the needs of the people and organisations they serve. The ways in which colleges impact upon individual learners, employers and their wider communities are also examined, along with issues of governance, leadership, and accountability. The report concludes that many colleges are deeply embedded within their communities, working independently and in partnership to facilitate access to learning for a wide range of individuals, including the hardest to reach. As a sector, they add considerable value to individuals, the economy and civil society. However, more could be gained if they extended their reach into communities and strengthened their community leadership.

Acknowledgements

The literature review was contributed by CFE, written by Lindsey Bowes, Alexandra Michael, Sarah Neat, and Sophie Spong. The authors would like to thank John Marriott, Bibliographic Researcher, International Centre for Guidance Studies (iCeGS), University of Derby, for his expert assistance with the searching and screening of the literature. We are also grateful to Nicola Underdown who jointly authored three of the stimulus papers which we have drawn upon in the production of this report. The team would like to thank Dr Jan Eldred for peer reviewing the literature review and for her helpful and constructive comments. We would finally like to thank the Inquiry Team, and Mark Ravenhall and Ian Yarroll in particular, for their ongoing support, as well as the Chair of the Commission, Baroness Sharp of Guilford, the Commissioners and Observers.

1 Introduction

The Inquiry into 'Colleges in Their Communities' was set up in January 2011. Its purpose was to investigate the role of, and public value added by, Further Education Colleges in order to develop a strategic vision for their future role in England.

This report has been produced by CFE and is submitted as evidence to the Inquiry into Colleges in Their Communities. It is based on a systematic review of the existing national and international literature on the Further Education (FE) sector. In this chapter we outline the background and context for the Inquiry and the approach taken for the systematic literature review.

Background

The Inquiry took place within a dynamic policy environment which led to the introduction of far-reaching changes to the skills system, including funding reforms and greater freedoms and responsibilities for Further Education Colleges (FECs) to shape and respond to local needs. The changes implemented by the Coalition Government recognised the important contribution FECs make to economic prosperity and social mobility as lead providers of education, training and skills to young people and adults. However, in the context of the 'Big Society', ministers were keen to explore the wider role colleges could play within the communities they serve.[1]

The independent Inquiry was chaired by Baroness Sharp of Guildford. The Commission comprised representatives from a wide range of stakeholder organisations including FECs, employers, unions, The Department for Business, Innovation and Skills (BIS), the Skills Funding Agency, Ofsted, The Learning and Skills Improvement Service (LSIS), the National Institute for Adult

---

1 Commission on Colleges in Their Communities (2011).

Continuing Education (NIACE), Association of Colleges (AoC) and 157 Group. CFE acted as the independent research partner to the project team led by NIACE and assumed responsibility for the systematic review of the literature.

Scope of the inquiry

The Inquiry project team conducted an initial scoping exercise to identify key issues and concerns. A total of seven thematic propositions were developed which provided the framework for the Inquiry.

1   A changed external environment demands new organisational models.
2   Colleges should be partners in the development of national adult learning policy.
3   Systems thinking is crucial to understanding the role of colleges in their communities.
4   Colleges are the learning experts in local economic planning.
5   The leadership development of college staff and governors needs to reflect the new challenges of colleges working in their communities.
6   Adult learners require an 'adult curriculum'.
7   Colleges should be the champions of an adult pedagogy for the 21st Century.

From these seven propositions, the following four key research questions were derived. These provided the framework for the evidence gathering process which comprised five elements: Commissioners' meetings; public call for evidence; expert seminar and visit programme; commissioned papers and a systematic literature review.

1   What is the relationship between colleges and their communities?
2   How do colleges contribute to local/community leadership? (i.e. as leaders of skills, as leaders in general, as trainers of leaders?)
3   How do colleges develop, implement and refine national adult learning policies and plans?
4   How do colleges define and arrive at an adult curriculum for their communities?

The literature review

The literature review set out to explore the existing relationship between colleges and their communities in order to develop a better understanding of how they currently contribute to local leadership and learning and skills policy, as well as the design and delivery of the adult curriculum. However, the literature review was undertaken in parallel with other aspects of the Inquiry and, as a result, the focus evolved as the Inquiry developed to centre on six key themes:

1   Business and employer voice
2   Civil society
3   Curriculum
4   Leadership
5   Learner voice
6   Local social and economic planning.

These thematic areas provided the focus for a series of expert seminars during which key stakeholders were invited to debate a number of questions. CFE produced and presented a paper based on the emerging findings from the literature review at each seminar in order to provide a stimulus for the discussion.[2] This report provides a synthesis of the key findings from the literature reviewed during the development of these thematic papers, supplemented by further evidence reviewed subsequently which focused in the main on international systems.

---

2   A report on the outcomes of the expert seminars, including all six thematic papers is available to download at: **www.niace.org.uk/current-work/colleges-in-their-communities-inquiry**

Approach

The literature review process comprised six inter-related stages:

- **Stage 1: Scoping.** During this first phase the key research questions for the literature review were developed, associated concepts and terminology were defined, and keywords and search terms were generated.
- **Stage 2: Searching.** This stage involved a comprehensive search for relevant primary sources of evidence using electronic databases and websites. The search concentrated on literature published in 2000 up to the end of August 2011. However, a small number of older texts have been included where the findings were judged to be pertinent and still relevant. The review was also primarily concerned to identify literature on FECs in England. However, the scope allowed for evidence from the rest of the United Kingdom and overseas to be included; a total of 11 other systems were examined in the timeframe available (see Chapter 2), selected to represent a cross-section of the models currently in operation.
- **Stage 3: Screening and selection.** The initial search identified a wide range of literature which was screened to ensure only papers that were relevant and within the scope of the review were selected.
- **Stage 4: Categorisation.** Once the relevant literature was selected, it was categorised thematically.
- **Stage 5: Analysis.** The evidence contained in the documents was extracted and analysed in order to address the key research questions.
- **Stage 6: Reporting.** The findings and key conclusions have been synthesised in this stand alone report for the Inquiry.

Although each of these stages was distinct, the overall process was iterative and designed to ensure that new evidence that came to light during the life of the Inquiry could be taken into account and significant emerging issues explored in more depth.

Definition of key terms

The FE sector in England is large and diverse. It was important to define which aspects of the sector the Inquiry was primarily concerned with at the outset in order to establish some clear parameters for the research.

College

In this context, FECs include General Further Education Colleges, Sixth Form Colleges, Land-based Colleges, Art, Design and Performing Arts Colleges (ADPAC), and Special Designated Colleges, which include Adult Residential Colleges.

Adult learning

Although FECs serve a range of learners of different ages, the prime interest of this Inquiry is adult learning, traditionally defined in funding terms, as learning for individuals aged 19 and over. The Inquiry takes a broad view of adult education, conceptualising it as a dynamic process which engages learners and learning professionals in the co-creation of knowledge, supports skills development and helps to create active citizens, rather than as simply 'adults on courses'.[3]

Communities

The term 'community' means different things to different people in different contexts and, as a result, a definitive definition has so far proved elusive. Defining 'community' in relation to FE is further complicated by the highly diverse nature of the sector. As a starting point, therefore, the term 'communities' rather than 'community' was adopted for the Inquiry to reflect the plurality of communities that colleges engage with. The term 'communities' is taken to mean specific groups of people bounded by a common interest and/or

---

3 Jackson, K. (1995), p. 188.

shared characteristics which could be personal, social, geographic and/or organisational.

This report

This report sets out the key findings from the systematic review of literature on colleges and their communities. It is illustrated throughout with case studies that have been developed to highlight some of the different and interesting ways in which education institutions (including higher education) are working with their communities in England and overseas[4].

The report is set out in eight chapters. Following this introduction, **Chapter 2** explores the notion of the 'Further Education College' in more depth by examining the different conceptualisations and manifestations of the FEC in the UK and internationally. **Chapter 3** provides a more detailed overview of recent skills policy and considers the challenges and opportunities for FECs in the current political and economic climate. **Chapter 4** examines the ways in which FECs engage with different communities at a strategic level in order to shape and identify their needs. **Chapter 5** considers how FECs are meeting the needs of their communities and considers the effectiveness of the models that are currently in place. **Chapter 6** examines the ways in which FECs are impacting on, and adding value to, their communities through an assessment of the evidence on the economic and social returns of adult education. **Chapter 7** considers the issues and challenges of accountability in the context of increased community engagement and reforms to funding and national targets. Current models, including the role of governance, are examined. The report concludes with **Chapter 8** which draws together the key messages for the Inquiry as well as identifying gaps in the evidence.

---

4 The case studies are not designed to be best practice but are illustrative only.

2 The FE college

When compared with their international counterparts, there is much about English FECs that is distinctive. The sector is highly diverse and, as a result, a typical college is difficult to define. Despite their differences, FECs are united in their commitment to improving the lives of the learners they serve

English FECs deliver a wide range of both publicly-funded and non-publicly funded provision to young people and adults on a full and part-time basis in a variety of formal and informal settings. In this chapter, we consider the composition and nature of this complex sector, including its purpose and mission. The devolved administrations of Scotland, Wales and Northern Ireland are responsible for developing local learning and skills policy as well as funding FE provision in their respective home nations. The similarities and differences between the models in operation in the United Kingdom will be explored, in addition to models operating in a range of other countries.

What is an FEC?

The vast majority of learners in the FE and skills sector study with an FEC; however, this group only represent a small proportion of the total number of organisations funded to deliver further education and training to young people and adults in England (23%).[5] The sector is comprised of 224 General Further Education and Tertiary Colleges (GFEC), 16 Land-based colleges (AHC); three Art, Design and Performing Arts Colleges (ADPAC), 94 Sixth Form Colleges (SFC) and 10 Specialist Designated Colleges (SDC).[6]

---

5 CFE (2011).
6 AoC (2011).

Historical development of FECs

The 1992 Further and Higher Education Act was a watershed moment in the evolution of the FE sector in England, and brought about substantive changes to the way FECs were funded and managed. Colleges were awarded incorporated status and, for the first time in almost a century, were freed from Local Education Authority (LEA) control. As self-governing organisations, they became accountable only to public funding bodies and government. Lines of local democratic accountability were weakened, and replaced by a model of local autonomy located within a national compliance framework. The changes promoted competition between colleges; although this undermined local partnership and co-operation, it also engendered innovation and entrepreneurial activity within colleges which helped to improve the way in which the curriculum was designed and delivered. However, the extent of entrepreneurial activity was hampered by the burden of top-down requirements, rigidity and regulation inherent in the new system.[7]

Currently colleges' activities are, in the main, funded and regulated by the Skills Funding Agency and the Young People's Learning Agency (YPLA). However, those that deliver Higher Education (HE) provision also receive direct funding from the Higher Education Funding Council for England (HEFCE). As autonomous institutions incorporated under statute, FECs are led by a principal or chief executive with support from a Senior Management Team and an independent Board of Governors. Governance structures vary depending on the size and nature of the college (see Chapter 7 for a fuller discussion of governance structures). As exempt charities, FECs are entitled to distinct financial benefits, such as rate and VAT relief.

Purpose and mission

Individual colleges develop their own strategic plans and associated objectives which are located within the regulatory framework set by

---

7 Howard, U. (2009).

the funding agencies on behalf of government. Despite their differing goals, colleges in England share some common overarching aims[8] to:

- widen participation amongst under-represented groups;
- help achieve academic progress;
- build vocational skills;
- support learning throughout life;
- promote social inclusion, cohesion and advancement; and
- contribute to the economy.

Colleges seek to achieve these aims through the development and delivery of flexible, accessible provision that supports the personal as well as the learning and skills needs of different learners. The primary purpose of FECs is, therefore, more than just the provision of qualifications; their mission is to widen participation, particularly amongst those groups that have been traditionally under-represented in non-compulsory education, and support them to achieve their potential. This includes enhancing learners' employability skills and preparing them for work in an increasingly global market[9] as well as promoting social inclusion, integration and cohesion by providing a neutral space in which diverse groups can learn together.[10] Intrinsically linked to the primary purpose of FECs is the contribution they make to the economy through the initial education of first time entrants to the workforce, the continuing professional development and training of those in employment, and as a major employer in their local area. The economic impact of FECs is considered in more depth in Chapter 6.

What do colleges do?

The FE sector is comprised of a range of organisations, many of which specialise in the delivery of particular types of provision.

---

8 Foster, A. (2005).
9 Rutter, J. (2010, pp.47-64).
10 Carpentieri, J. D. and Vorhaus, J. (2010).

However, colleges are distinct in providing a wide range of opportunities such as adult, community and work-based learning, Basic Skills, and ESOL[11] in addition to academic and vocational qualifications, including higher education.

In 2009-10, the number of learners studying in England's colleges totalled 3.4 million.[12] During the same period, colleges were responsible for delivering:

- A quarter of all Apprenticeships.
- Over two-fifths (41%) of all vocational qualifications.
- 14 per cent of informal adult and community learning.
- 38 per cent of entrants to higher education.
- 78 per cent of HNCs, 59 per cent of HNDs and half of all Foundation Degrees which amounts to a 12 per cent share of the HE market.[13]

Much of the formal and/or accredited learning delivered by FECs is designed to address the skills challenges facing the UK: in 2010, one in ten adults aged 20 to retirement had no qualifications; approximately 50% of the working age population lacked basic numeracy skills; one in six lacked basic literacy skills[14]; and, in May 2011, 2.45 million people were unemployed.[15] However, informal adult and community learning is also integral to the latest skills strategy, located within the wider framework of the 'Big Society'. It is the Coalition Government's belief that access to informal learning will help ensure citizens are able to engage effectively in civil society and contribute more fully to their local community as well as the economy.[16] Moving forward, colleges, along with other providers, may be expected to offer more of these types of opportunities, which range from arts, culture and health to digital skills, employability skills, family learning, civic engagement and community development.

---

11 English for Speakers of Other Languages.
12 AoC (2010).
13 King, M., Widdowson, J. and Brown, R. (2008).
14 The Poverty Site (2011).
15 Office for National Statistics (2011).
16 BIS (2010e).

Although much college provision is delivered by college staff, there is evidence that colleges are increasingly collaborating with employers and other providers in both the public and the private sectors. In addition, colleges are represented on a number of partnerships and work with a variety of organisations in order to tackle wider social and economic issues. It is consequently difficult to explore 'what colleges do' in isolation but rather as an important part of a wider network or ecosystem. This is explored further in Chapters 5 and 6.

Who do colleges serve?

FECs serve a wide range of learners; however widening participation amongst traditionally under-represented groups is at the heart of the FE sector's mission, and the mission of FECs in particular. As a result, the profile of the learners engaged with colleges is highly diverse:[17]

- 19% of students in colleges describe themselves as belonging to a minority ethnic group, compared with 12% of the general population.
- 80% of ESOL students study at a college.
- 3% of college students are aged over 60.
- FE is the main provider for post-16 learners with learning difficulties and/or disabilities.[18]
- 29% of learners in General FECs are from relatively disadvantaged postcode areas compared to 25% of the whole population.[19]

First and foremost, therefore, colleges exist to serve their learners and the communities they represent, both personally and professionally. The extent and nature of the communities served will vary depending on the college; while some are predominantly defined in geographical terms, others are distinguished along sectoral lines. It is common for learners to be drawn from across local authority boundaries, and this is especially the case for large colleges and specialist institutions that

---

17   AoC (2010).
18, 19   Foster, A. (2005).

work at a national level.[20] College communities are, therefore, incredibly diverse, as Dick Palmer of City College in Norwich recently noted:

> "...the idea of the local FE college, with a strong orientation towards local community and the local economy, might appear somewhat outdated...success in the modern world crucially depends upon understanding the nuances in national, regional, local and even micro markets. We all operate in settings that are simultaneously global and local."[21]

However, colleges must also satisfy a range of other stakeholders including: government and the funding agencies; Ofsted; Sector Skills Councils; Local Authorities; and employers. Recent reductions in bureaucracy and top-down targets, along with the drive for greater engagement with local communities and skills policy development, has implications for the relationship between FECs and these different stakeholder groups. These present the sector with a number of key challenges in relation to leadership and management, governance, and accountability in particular. These themes will be explored in more depth throughout this report.

International models

As we consider the role of FECs in England and the opportunities for their future development, it is important to look at other models, systems and processes. We examined models of FE and the role of colleges in 11 countries in the time available, selected for the insights they provided into the English system. Skills policy and the funding of FE are devolved to each of the home nations in the UK and as a result different systems have emerged that reflect the local social, economic and political circumstances. We, therefore, examine these systems before moving on to consider the similarities and differences

---

20 AoC (2008).
21 Palmer, D. (2009) .

between the English system and the systems in operation in other English speaking countries, such as Australia, Canada and the United States. Finally, we study the systems in operation in five European countries which contrast with England in terms of governance, funding and focus.

The UK

Northern Ireland

The Department for Employment and Learning (DELNI) has responsibility for FE in Northern Ireland which is delivered by six multi-campus colleges alongside school sixth forms. Like English FECs, these colleges have charitable status and benefit from certain exemptions from capital gains tax and income and corporation taxes. The strategic objectives of the FE sector are to:

- support regional economic development and, in particular, provide the skills necessary for the knowledge-based economy;
- increase participation and widen access to those previously under-represented in the sector; and
- improve the quality of provision and enhance standards of performance. [22]

Colleges deliver a wide range of provision which includes vocational and academic qualifications at Levels 2 and 3 and Higher Education. They serve 180,000 students at any one time and deliver FE to one in three 16-18 year olds. There are currently over 12,000 students undertaking HE in FE which amounts to 18 per cent of all HE delivered in Northern Ireland. Combined, they have a turnover of £250 million.[23]

The six colleges were formed in 2007 as a result of a series of mergers between 16 FE providers. They now operate across over 40

---

22 Department for Employment and Learning (2011).
23 Northern Ireland Assembly (2011).

campuses and through over 400 outreach community locations.[24] The Minister for Employment and Learning, Sir Reg Empey said: *"The introduction of six 'super' colleges is excellent news for Northern Ireland's education sector and will have a significant impact for learners, the community and local businesses. Working with their economic and educational partners, the new colleges will be at the forefront of ensuring that Northern Ireland has the necessary skills to compete in a modern, knowledge based, global economy."*[25] The mergers have enabled the colleges to make efficiency savings of 20 per cent, whilst the number of students has increased.[26]

Following the incorporation of FECs in England four years earlier, FECs in Northern Ireland were freed from Education and Library Board control in 1997 and set up as free-standing incorporated organisations managed by a governing body appointed by DELNI. The role of the governing body is similar to that in English FECs. They are responsible for the overall functioning of the college and ensure that delivery is suitable and efficient for learners. Governors are responsible for agreeing and monitoring the college's strategy and provide strategic leadership.[27] The composition of governing bodies in Northern Ireland is diverse. At least half of governors must be drawn from the private sector; other members include the college principal, up to two staff members, one student, two people with an interest in education or community activities and up to two co-opted by existing members.

DELNI is responsible for setting the strategic direction for, and financing of, the FE system in Northern Ireland but each individual college develops its own curriculum and strategy within this framework.[28] Funding is allocated through the Funded Learning Unit [FLU] model. The Department agrees with the college the maximum amount and type of provision to be funded. The FLU Distributive Mechanism is then used to convert the actual and planned provision into Funded Learning Units to determine allocations and monitor a college's performance. Colleges are not, however, given a minimum number

24   Colleges Northern Ireland (2011).
25   Department for Employment and Learning (2011).
26   Northern Ireland Assembly (2011).
27   Department for Employment and Learning (2008)].

of qualifications which they must deliver. Further funding is provided to colleges to enable them to widen access, increase participation, address skills shortages and align provision under the Department's Strategy.

The Department's 2006 strategy *FE Means Business* underlined the importance of collaboration and partnership between the statutory FE sector and voluntary and community organisations to ensure the needs of the wider community are met. Colleges are extensively involved in partnerships with schools to deliver enhancements to the 14-19 curriculum. They also offer a range of courses in partnership with post-primary schools to deliver technical and professional courses, including National and First Diplomas. All colleges have dedicated business development units which engage with employers and the different departments within the college. It is estimated that they are currently engaging with approximately 4,500 businesses.

Colleges Northern Ireland acts as the representative body for the sector. Its vision is: *"To support, represent and promote the colleges and positively impact upon their vital contribution to Northern Ireland's economic and social well-being."*[29] It is made up of two people from each college, who are accountable to the colleges and undertake a range of functions including: engaging with a range of stakeholders; supporting the Management Information System which is used by all six colleges and is jointly funded by all colleges and the Department; and supporting ongoing projects.

A number of strengths can be identified in this model. Condensing provision into just six FECs is cost efficient and has enabled good practice to be shared and operations to be improved. Although governance is fairly similar to that in England, each college has more autonomy to innovate and develop their own teaching strategy which is underpinned with funding that looks forward rather than back. Similar to many other countries, widening access and community engagement is central to their activity, with an impressive number of employers already engaged. That said, there are also limitations in this approach. The establishment of 'super colleges' could reduce

---

28 Department for Employment and Learning (2011).
29 Colleges Northern Ireland (2011).

opportunities to study niche subjects often taught at more specialist institutions. Furthermore, the close-knit community that distinguishes the small college is likely lost within a larger institutional structure.

Scotland

The Scottish lifelong learning strategy aims to ensure learners develop the attributes, knowledge and skills they need for learning, life, and work.[30] There are 43 FECs in Scotland, which cater for a population of approximately five million. They offer a diverse curriculum that includes vocational, further and higher education, and which is delivered in a flexible way. There are approximately 350,000 learners in Scotland's colleges.[31] As a result of their geographical spread, these learners and their communities are incredibly diverse. Consequently the sector also plays an important role in the Scottish Government's social inclusion agenda.[32]

Qualifications at the secondary and further education level are provided by the national awarding and accrediting body in Scotland - the Scottish Qualification Authority. Following compulsory education, pupils can stay on at school to take Higher or Advanced Higher exams, or pursue vocational qualifications at FECs which include SVQs, Higher National Certificates and Higher National Diplomas. Pupils who decide to take Higher and Advanced Higher exams can enrol at Scottish universities after completing one year and embark on four year degrees, or they can spend an additional year taking further Higher and Advanced Higher exams before entering higher education. Pupils who follow the vocational route often spend the first two years studying for a HND at a FEC before embarking on their university career.[33, 34]

As in other parts of the UK, Scottish colleges are led by a principal and a governing board which is selected to reflect the diversity of the

30 The Scottish Government (2011b).
31 Kidner, C. (2011).
32 The Scottish Government (2011a).
33 Wikipedia (2011c).
34 Wikipedia (2011b).

sector and the communities served by the college. Alongside college principals, the board is ultimately responsible for the colleges' leadership, strategic direction, reputation, and financial health. It is also responsible for: the well-being of staff and students; establishing high standards of academic conduct; monitoring the quality of provision; and compliance with the statutes, ordinances and provisions regulating the college and its framework of governance.[35]

Colleges receive the majority of their funding from the Scottish Funding Council (SFC) and quality of their provision is reviewed by Her Majesty's Inspectorate of Education every four years.[36] Colleges are allocated funding in blocks, which is determined by the SFC through weighted sums formulas. Courses and modules are assigned particular weights according to the number of credits and hours of learning attached to them. Colleges then distribute the funding across departments and courses as they see fit. This enables them to respond to national, regional, local and institutional priorities.[37]

Although the government provides a framework for learning and teaching, the responsibility for what is delivered within colleges rests with the educational institutions.[38] Scotland has explicitly eschewed qualification targets because, as a nation, it has already achieved high attainment levels when compared to England. The focus in Scotland is on the utilisation and impact of skills.[39]

Scottish colleges, like Welsh institutions, are subject to relatively light-touch management. Although targets play their part within the performance framework, colleges are regarded as essentially self-regulating. However, Scottish colleges have robust internal monitoring and performance structures for staff which have earned them this autonomy.[40] In addition, a recent review powerfully reinforced the

---

35   CIPFA and Scotland's Colleges (2010).
36   Kidner, C. (2011).
37   Brown, D., Hughes, T. and Fletcher, T. (2010).
38   The Scottish Government (2011b).
39, 40 Brown, D., Hughes, T. and Fletcher, T. (2010).

idea that quality assurance was a collective responsibility.[41]

There is a strong culture of collaboration within Scottish colleges. Frequent dialogue and partnership occurs across the sector, and between colleges and community groups, various sector bodies, local authorities and the central administration.[42] Colleges are also represented by 'Scotland's Colleges', an organisation that speaks on behalf of colleges to policymakers and further supports this collaborative approach.[43] However, it should be noted that there are a relatively small number of colleges in Scotland when compared to England, which makes collaborative working and direct dialogue with policymakers much easier.[44]

In order to understand and respond to the emerging needs of their communities, college tutors and leaders fulfil a key role in identifying shifts in skills requirements, changes in patterns of employment and/or in economic migration. In addition, learner enquiries also provide insight into skills needs. Colleges pass these messages back up the chain to policymakers to produce system-level readjustments and inform policy and resource allocation.[45] However, tensions in the system are created when the demand from employers or learners for a particular course outstrips the colleges' capacity to deliver because funding is capped. As a result, some courses are unable to expand.[46]

Supporting social inclusion, catering for community needs, and responding to local and national priorities are all key strengths of the Scottish model. In addition, the progressive funding model enables colleges to respond to the needs of the local labour market and establish trusting relationships with employers. However, funding constraints limit their capacity to respond to substantial increases in demand for new and existing provision. Strong quality assurance and performance management measures ensure the success of a light-touch management approach which helps to foster both a high degree of individual autonomy and effective inter-college collaboration.

41, 42   James, D. (2011).
43   Kidner, C. (2011).
44, 45   James, D. (2011).
46   Brown, D., Hughes, T. and Fletcher, T. (2010).

Wales

In Wales, further education is delivered by a range of organisations including FECs, Sixth Form Colleges and public, private and voluntary sector training providers. Welsh learners have the choice to embark upon vocational courses, A-levels or the Welsh Baccalaureate Qualification (WBQ). The WBQ runs alongside and complements qualifications such as A-levels but can also be taken at an earlier stage alongside GCSEs.

There are 19 FECs in Wales serving a population of approximately three million. As in other parts of the UK, each institution is led by a principal and governed by a body that is representative of the area it serves. The range and type of provision on offer also reflects that delivered in the other home nations and includes: academic and vocational qualifications, leisure learning and training. The Learning and Skills Measure which is expected to be fully operational by 2012 will ensure that colleges provide a range of vocational and academic courses for young people aged 14-16 and those up to the age of 19.[47]

FECs are largely funded by the Department for Children, Education, Lifelong Learning and Skills (DCELLS) of the Welsh Assembly Government (WAG). Thee provide colleges with an annual volume-based target on learner activities. However, monitoring of college activities is relatively light-touch; targets are viewed as ambitions so that colleges are free to respond to changes in demand by shifting the balance of provision towards growing subject areas. This hands-off approach means that there is less of a focus on qualification output and, as such, colleges are afforded more freedom to set their own priorities and targets.[48]

The Welsh inspectorate, Estyn, operates a framework that is similar to that in England but viewed as less inquisitorial and more supportive.[49] However, it is important to note that colleges in Wales, like Scotland, have their own robust internal monitoring and performance structures which include the monitoring of completion and retention

---

47 National Assembly for Wales (2009).
48 Brown, D., Hughes, T. and Fletcher, T. (2010).
49 James, D. (2011).

rates, as well as attainment for each course.[50] This positive regard for quality regime is being further developed by ColegauCymru (Colleges Wales), the national organisation representing all FECs and institutions in Wales, who are hoping to develop a model of self-regulation for colleges.[51]

Welsh colleges operate in a collaborative environment and work with each other, schools, other training providers and higher education institutions (HEIs) to find more efficient and effective ways of organising provision for the benefit of learners. This is facilitated by the high prevalence of socialist values and cooperative endeavour; the existence of policy-framed expectations and possibilities for collaboration between colleges and other providers; and high levels of direct dialogue between colleges and policymakers. ColegauCymru helps to contribute to this environment by acting as a single vehicle for colleges to work together and share good practice. However, it should also be noted that in contrast to England, there is a relatively small number of colleges operating in Wales, which make collaborative working and direct dialogue with policymakers much easier.[52]

Following the recommendations of a recent report, greater emphasis will be placed on collaboration and partnership working with a view to creating more learning opportunities in FE. The report also proposes that a new social enterprise-type model of governance for FECs should be established and more colleges should merge.[53] John Graystone, Chief Executive of ColegauCymru asserted:

"I am pleased that the report recognises that FE colleges are keen to collaborate with others for the benefit of learners and that it notes the determination within the FE sector to develop more opportunities for learning through the medium of Welsh... Colleges have been working with an increasingly wide range of partners over recent years to raise quality through making savings through sharing services with others in order to protect and improve front line education services...

50 Brown, D., Hughes, T. and Fletcher, T. (2010).
51 James, D. (2011).
52 James, D. (2011).
53 Humphreys, R. (2001).

A ColegauCymru survey on shared services shows colleges have each saved more than £100,000 per year."[54]

John Graystone, Chief Executive of ColegauCymru

The Welsh system shares many strengths and characteristics with the Scottish system including: a diversity of providers and study options; representative governing bodies; and an emphasis on robust quality assurance and self-regulation. Funding is flexible and enables providers to respond effectively to shifts in demand. Collaboration and partnership is a key feature of the system, facilitated by the size of the sector and the opportunities for direct dialogue and exchange between providers and policymakers.

Australia

The Australian FE system is, in many respects, closest to the system operating in England. The current government also shares many of the UK's political ambitions for the FE sector; however, Australia is not currently experiencing the same economic challenges facing Europe and the United States.

The Department of Education, Science and Training (DEST) is responsible for Australia's education and training system. DEST works through numerous agencies which collaborate with State and Territory governments, other Commonwealth agencies, industry, and contracted service providers to develop education and training policy as well as provide advice and guidance.

A range of organisations provide FE in Australia, including technical colleges; private training providers, community groups, group training companies and enterprises.[55] The term 'college' is used to refer to a number of different types of provider including some tertiary institutions, such as medical or art schools, and certain secondary schools teaching pupils aged 12-18. However, more generally the term 'college' is applied to post-secondary institutions that offer predominantly vocational education programmes, undertaken in pursuit of

---

54 ColegauCymru (2011).
55 Goozee, G. (2001).

higher level study or employment-based qualifications and training.[56]

Technical and Further Education (TAFE) colleges are Australia's largest post-secondary provider. More than 230 TAFE colleges now exist, with 84 institutes operating over 300 campuses around the country.[57] Funded mostly by the State and Commonwealth Government, eight different State or Territory authorities regulate the system. In contrast to the UK, control of the system is becoming increasingly centralised.[58]

The TAFE system has been compared to the UK model because of its distinct remit from the school sector. TAFE colleges provide vocational education as well as a 'stepping stone' to university level studies and have experienced considerable growth in the past few years.[59] TAFE courses primarily enable students to develop workplace skills for specific occupations within the technical, government and business sectors. As in England, industry standards are used to ensure programmes equip students with the competencies they need before they enter employment. Those already in employment can also study TAFE courses in order to advance their skill set and enhance their career prospects. Like English colleges, most students study part-time, combining employment and study, either on campus or by distance learning. More recently, some TAFE colleges have been exploring more innovative ways to deliver programmes, including via technology or in the work place.[60] Also mirroring the APEL[61] system in operation in some FECs and HEIs in England, TAFE colleges recognise expertise gained through work and can award credit where appropriate.[62]

Also reflecting changes in English skills policy is the drive to establish an industry-led system in Australia which ensures training meets employers' needs. Apprenticeships are now a key feature of both the Australian and English FE sectors. To encourage take-up of appren-

---

56 Australian Education Network (2011).
57 Goozee, G. (2001).
58 Leney, T., May, T., Hayward, G. and Wilde, S. (2007).
59 Australian Education Network (2011).
60 Goozee, G. (2001).
61 Accreditation of prior and experiential learning
62 The IEA College of TAFE (2011)].

tices, incentives are paid to employers once the apprentice has completed their course. However, this policy is being reviewed to avoid employers poaching apprentices from businesses that invest heavily in training by splitting the incentive payments. Despite significant reforms to the Australian system, a number of issues have been identified in relation to the implementation of policies designed to improve economic outcomes. Incentive strategies, such as the one discussed above, and training levies seem to be too easily used to remedy challenges in the system.[63]

Given the many similarities between the Australian and English system, it will be interesting to observe how the Australian model evolves and what further enhancements can be made while operating in a stable economic climate. Diversity of provision and flexibility of delivery are two key strengths of this system; another is the focus on vocational skills taught in the workplace, according to industry standards and supported by employers within an increasingly industry-led environment. Nonetheless, Australia needs to review the use of incentive schemes to drive changes in policy and behaviour to avoid an ongoing over-reliance on government intervention and funding in the sector.

North America

United States of America

The American Community College has long since been held up as a model of good practice and an example of how institutions can successfully serve 'the top 100 per cent' of learners within their local community. In 2009, Dougherty claimed that the US Community College could *"provide an illuminating comparison for the British FE college"*, given that, despite the disparities between the two systems, there are several similarities in their roles and aims within society.[64]

---

63 Leney, T., May, T., Hayward, G. and Wilde, S. (2007).
64 Widdowson, J. (2010).

With over 1,000 Community Colleges in the US, these public, two-year institutions play an important role in the country's education system. The predominant feature of these colleges is that they provide opportunities for less-advantaged students to undertake vocational training as well as graduate level courses, including the four year Baccalaureate degree. Many students who pursue the Baccalaureate now start their studies at a Community College before progressing onto a four year college or university to complete the final years of their programme. In some states progression agreements between two and four year colleges are mandated in law, facilitating seamless progression for learners.[65] More recently, a number of Community Colleges have begun to offer their own Baccalaureate degrees, although state approval must be sought before this can occur. In contrast with English FECs, American Community Colleges are regarded as an integral element of the HE system. Programmes are rarely considered an end in their own right, but rather a stepping stone to a degree.[66]

Also in contrast with England, the federal government has very little involvement with the college sector, providing just 14% of their revenue. Instead, it is the state and local government which maintain control over Community Colleges, determining if and where they should be established and how they are run. As a result, colleges vary significantly across the country and diverse roles are played by the state.

In line with the policy direction that the UK Government is currently pursuing, American Community Colleges focus on meeting the needs of their communities (both in terms of their initial education and continued professional development). As such, they provide a diverse suite of qualifications and courses to supply the local economy with newly trained or re-skilled vocational and 'middle' or 'semi-professional' workers. In addition, their widespread locations and willingness to take on all types of student makes them a popular choice for many who believe studying at university is not a viable option. Colleges are also widely used for

---

65 Amey, M. J., Eddy, P. L. and Campbell, T. G. (2010).
66 King, M., Widdowson, J. and Brown, R. (2008).

adult, continuing and community education. Although the state provides some funding for this type of activity, they impose fewer regulations and restrictions, enabling new course offerings to be explored and developed in response to local labour market needs.[67]

The US has made great strides in widening access and participation to FE as well engaging local communities. While the US model should be applauded for embracing individuals from all backgrounds and abilities, giving them an opportunity to up-skill and progress, the evidence suggests that many of these students have complex needs and often fail to complete their studies. Currently, almost 50% of students leave without actually gaining a qualification. In addition, while decentralised governance allows for greater experimentation and local autonomy, individual state control results in significant variation in levels of resources and funding across the country. This has serious implications for the quality of the student learning experience and parity between qualifications gained from different colleges in different parts of the country. [68]

Canada

The Canadian system is similar to the United States in that FE and Community Colleges are established by individual states and provinces. We noted above that a key strength of this approach is the flexibility it affords colleges to respond to local need, but that the lack of standardisation has implications for the quality and consistency of learning provision.[69]

As in England and elsewhere, most Canadian Community Colleges serve the needs of multiple groups and deliver a range of provision. Primarily, they offer academic programmes for students en route to university and occupational programmes for those in or seeking to enter the workforce. For those wishing to pursue higher level education, some colleges (University Community Colleges) deliver the first two years of a bachelors' degree, after which a student can transfer

---

67, 68 Dougherty, K. J. (2010).
69   Grubb, W. N. (2003).

to a university to complete their studies. Canadian Community Colleges cater for adults as well as young people. Provision includes: evening and weekend courses designed to up-skill working adults, particularly those who are looking for a career change; bespoke training for employers; recreational courses for adults; literacy programmes; and 'second chance' programmes to help adults who have been out of work for some time to re-enter employment.

Many colleges also provide services or activities for the wider community. These include supporting economic development (see case study of Niagara College in Chapter 6); advising small businesses about industry practices; facilitating industry networks and collaboration; identifying business development opportunities for local employers; and targeting provision at specific industry needs to attract new business to an area. Furthermore, colleges are also engaged in 'community development' activities and help to tackle issues faced by the community through 'task forces'.[70]

Regardless of age or purpose of study, students are well supported in Canada. New students are helped to integrate into the student community, and many institutions provide a variety of student services and extra-curricular activities on campus.

College fees in Canada are generally less than a thousand dollars, which is much lower than those charged by the universities; however, the level depends on the state or province in which the college is situated. Quebec has adopted a funding approach that requires employers to contribute to a training tax fund or offer training themselves. Although this approach was initially received with some hostility by employers, it is now accepted as a positive way to stimulate discussions between partners.

As the drive towards co-financing gathers pace in England, lessons from the Canadian experience could usefully be learned. A particular strength of this model includes the practical hands-on approach taken by colleges to engage businesses through facilitation activities. Not only does this help support the local economy but it also ensures the colleges' commercial customer base is developed. A further strength

---

70 Ibid.

is the wide range of provision offered and the strong support provided for a relatively low cost.

Western Europe and Scandinavia

The FE systems operating in Europe provide an interesting comparison for the English system. Here we present five examples drawn from some of the UK's competitor nations.

Sweden

In contrast to the industry-led models of England and Australia, the Swedish approach to FE is primarily concerned with achieving wider societal and personal development goals.[71] Adult and compulsory education falls under the remit of the *Skolverket* agency. As an intermediary between the central ministry and local authorities, it assumes responsibility for performance management and quality assurance, as well as supporting teacher training and school management.[72] This responsibility cascades down to the 288 local authorities and 23 county councils; the former is then allocated government funding for education, which is mainly sourced from income taxes and varies in amount dependent on a municipality's population and age profile. In recent years, an objectives and results driven system has replaced its former model of strict regulation and centralisation.[73]

All teachers work towards the same teaching certificate, which recognises any prior learning and experience they may have. Once qualified, teachers are then employed directly by their local authority which base teacher salaries on length of service rather than professional qualifications.[74] Governance changes over time have resulted in greater decision making power and responsibility for leaders. For example, within each school, the head teacher determines the school plan, before it is monitored and assessed by its municipal body. However, collaboration is also a key feature of the Swedish system. Qualifications and curricula are generally developed through part-

71 Leney, T., May, T., Hayward, G. and Wilde, S. (2007).
72 UNESCO-UNEVOC (1998).
73 Lundahl, L. (2002).

nership working between different levels of schools (i.e. compulsory and post-compulsory) businesses, industry representative bodies, and teachers' associations.

Unlike the UK, there are no institutional divisions between FECs, sixth form colleges and school sixth forms.[75] Furthermore there are no distinctions between general education and vocational training; these have been integrated and are now studied together. That said, vocational courses are important in Sweden. Apprenticeship programmes are in place and continuing vocational education is strongly supported financially by employers, who also provide workplace learning opportunities.

Individuals in Sweden are encouraged to pursue further education and up-skill themselves. Learning subsidies and loans are provided as well as other incentives to progress further in education. Employees are also supported should they decide to undertake further learning; the majority of adult education is free, employees are entitled to study leave, and those with a good employment record can take advantage of special support. However, research suggests that employer participation overall needs to increase to bring working life and academia closer together.[76]

A number of strengths can be identified within the Swedish model. The emphasis placed on quality assurance and performance management helps drive the system and has effectively replaced the previous model of centralised controls. Collaboration is key and there are good examples of partnerships between different schools as well as with industry. Vocational courses – in particular Apprenticeships – are well supported by employers and a continuous learning culture with financial support is well embedded. Perhaps as a result of this focus on the importance of learning, Sweden is now ranked as the second most competitive economy in the world[77] and predicted to become a talent

74   Drakenberg, M. (2001).
75, 76 Leney, T., May, T., Hayward, G. and Wilde, S. (2007).
77   Schwab, K. (ed.) (2010).

magnet for the world's most purposeful workers.[78] However, the success of the system comes at a cost - tax in Sweden is nearly double the rate in the United States and Ireland and is at a level that could not be envisaged in the UK at this time.[79]

Finland

Finland is another country which has made significant changes to its educational system over recent years. Previously all types and stages of education were controlled by detailed legislation; however, decentralisation of control over a decade ago has created a model which empowers local authorities, educational and vocational providers to take greater responsibility. Although minimum statutory requirements are in place around student education and support, as long as providers meet these requirements, they are free to develop learning programmes and allocate public funding as they wish.

Like Sweden, Finland provides substantial support for individuals who wish to continue studying. Funding is available for all stages of education, from school through to higher education. As a result, Finland has often been referred to as one of the highest European performers given its 'cradle-to-grave' approach to lifelong learning for its citizens.[80]

Significant funding is also invested in vocational colleges to ensure they stay up-to-date, and are innovative and appealing to students and employers. Again, similar to Sweden, vocational qualifications are developed through a collaborative process involving local and national government, teachers and lecturers, businesses and employer representative bodies. Corporate and representative governance is strongly encouraged through these partnership arrangements.[81]

Many Finnish vocational colleges have merged with other colleges over time to become polytechnics, with both secondary and tertiary courses on offer. More recently, some of these polytechnics have trialled new post-graduate degrees, targeting students who have

---

78,79   Wikipedia (2011).
80   Leney, T., May, T., Hayward, G. and Wilde, S. (2007).
81   Ibid.

undertaken at least three years' work experience following a poly-technic or HE degree.

Teachers in vocational colleges are required to have gained a suit-able polytechnic or HE degree as well as undertaking a year (or 35 credits) of pedagogical studies and three years experience within a related area. One of the ongoing development areas for teachers has been identified as school management training.

Similar to Sweden in many ways, Finland places a great deal of emphasis on collaborative working, significant government invest-ment in learning and greater freedom and autonomy for providers. As in Northern Ireland, college mergers have led to greater efficiencies and opportunities for studying a wide range of qualifications and individuals are well supported. However, there appears to be less focus on supporting the wider community and engaging them in activities beyond the core curriculum.

Germany

Like in the USA and Canada, Germany's individual federated states assume main responsibility for education. Adult education and continuing education are provided through a wide range of institu-tions, controlled by diverse organisations including: Trade Unions; company-based groups; religious institutes; commercial groups; and distance learning operator amongst others. The state controls and funds some institutions, others are commercially run and funded through the private economy, sponsors, households and the Federal Labour Agency.[82]

In contrast to the models in North America and England, the German FE system has traditionally been less concerned with univer-sity level courses, instead focusing on vocational training and skilled apprenticeships.[83] Many occupations in Germany require vocational skills and as a result the *duales system* (dual system) was established to enable students to complete their training in a vocational school or college as well as in the workplace. A key strength of this approach

---

82 Nuissl, E. and Pehl, K. (2004).
83 Wikipedia (2011d).

is that learners have the opportunity to apply the skills they have learned in a practical setting. This model is a joint initiative between government and industry. Vocational education in public vocational schools is funded by the federal government and the Laender, whilst training companies and businesses cover the costs of workplace training.[84] Approximately two-thirds of students in Germany undertake this type of vocational training in a two to three year period.[85] Beyond vocational training, continuing education is in a niche of its own, building on the knowledge, skills and experience that an individual has already acquired. Given the increasing demand for continuing education, the needs of the economy are generally prioritised.

There are a number of benefits associated with the German system which include: a reduced financial burden on the state; considerable collaboration between the government and industry; and the development of a skilled workforce trained in specialist vocational areas. However, there is a risk that focusing on a sole area of expertise may impact on social mobility and reduce opportunities to transfer across different careers. Moreover, those that find themselves in a redundancy situation may find it difficult to find new roles without undertaking further training because of their narrowly specialised skills. Another interesting dimension to the German model is that competition between institutions has been discouraged in an attempt to equalise quality.[86] This is in contrast to current policy in England which actively encourages competition between institutions and penalises under-performance.

The Netherlands

The Minister of Education, Culture and Science together with The Netherlands' municipal governments are responsible for Dutch education policy. Following five years of secondary school, students can pursue further education in three ways: by studying middle-level vocational education; through higher professional or vocational

84   Hippach-Schneider, U., Krause, M. and Woll, C. (2007).
85   Huisman, J. (2003).
86   Grubb, W. N. (2003).

education; and third, by undertaking scientific education.[87] The former study route is considered to be secondary education and is comparable to the community college approach.[88] Most subjects allow for either full or part-time study.

The Netherlands' 43 colleges provide for a population of 16 million; this is a significant task when compared to Scotland where the same number of colleges serves a population of just five million people.[89] A key challenge for the sector is improving the quality of teaching following reports that 50,000 18-23 year olds drop out.[90] As a result, lecturers' skills, continuous professional development and teaching approaches are being scrutinised more closely by government. However, colleges are well supported by employers – who are incentivised by government to offer work placements for full-time students – as well as the government directly, from which they receive 95% of their income. That said, as a result of this majority funding approach, colleges in the Netherlands are yet to establish a commercial side.

Although the Netherlands' FECs are stretched to provide for their high number of students, the provision offered is varied and flexible. That said, quality assurance has been poor in the past leading to many students leaving their studies without achieving. Evidence suggests that increased government intervention will need to be considered carefully given that previous incentive plans provided to colleges have reduced their inclination to pursue separate income streams.

Denmark

An entirely different model of education can be seen in the Danish system, where school attendance is not mandatory; instead individuals are only obliged to undertake 'some form of education'. One of the ways in which they 'educate' adults between 18 and 24 is through their Danish Folk High Schools. These institutions, described as the *"most original contribution Denmark has made to international*

87   British Council (2007).
88   Fulbright Center (2011).
89, 90 Munro, N. (2009).

thinking about popular education" provide informal learning opportunities during a four month average residential stay.[91]

Obliged to provide a 'general broadening education', these Folk High Schools focus predominantly on learning about life. Unlike traditional specialist educational colleges, they have complete autonomy and freedom to design their courses and programmes. In fact there are no entry requirements and no exams or coursework during the stay; a 'proof of attendance' diploma is simply provided at the end of the four months. Professional and dedicated teachers take a collaborative approach to their lessons, encouraging supportive learning, discussion and debate to help students identify and enhance their own skills sets. Around 50,000 adults have attended these schools during the past few years.[92]

The Ministry of Education approves these schools' regulations and statutes. State funding provides approximately 50% of the schools' income; student fees and facility hire provides the remainder income. Each school's democratic base determines who should sit on the Board, which is then responsible for deciding the philosophical approach, strategic direction and principal – who is responsible for the operational management of the school along with the teaching staff. Only the Board can decide to establish or terminate one of these schools; the authorities have no control.[93]

The politics of the Danish Folk High Schools reflect the EU's policy on education with its emphasis on lifelong learning. Similar types of further education schools can be found in other parts of Scandinavia and Germany, although the Swedish and German schools are more closely aligned to the formal educational system. France also has a similar model; its Université Populaire resembles the Danish Model.[94]

The Danish focus on the learning experience helps to develop rounded individuals who learn life skills in addition to the core curriculum and specific subjects. The complete autonomy held by individual schools also enables a tailored approach to be adopted, allowing individuals to choose which school is most appropriate for them. However, the potential downsides of this approach are that

---

91, 92, 93, 94 Andresén A., Kværndrup, S. and Glahn, N. (2010).

progress made by students and the skills and competencies they develop may be hard to measure and compare with students from other institutions. Furthermore, there appears to be little connection to industry – either to prepare students for the workforce or engage businesses as customers.

Summary

The review of international models of FE has revealed a rich diversity of approaches, none of which are directly comparable to the English system. Although all have evolved and continue to operate in dynamic political and economic environments, the emphasis placed on issues such as widening access, employer engagement and social and personal development varies considerably. For example, colleges in the USA are principally concerned with widening access; although many English colleges are also committed to this principle, they, along with FE providers in Australia, place a great deal of emphasis on the role of industry in shaping the system. In contrast, Scandinavian models are concerned with wider societal and personal development in addition to skills. Differing approaches to collaboration and competition are also identified. For example, in Germany provision is highly specialised and competition between institutions is actively discouraged to ensure parity and consistency across the sector; in the devolved administrations of the UK collaboration amongst colleges operating in is widespread. Current skills policy in England is focussed on driving up the number of apprenticeships and places increased emphasis on the role of colleges in supporting and promoting social inclusion and mobility. However, in contrast to other nations, these objectives are to be achieved in an environment where colleges can be simultaneously collaborators and competitors.

Despite these differences, many of the models also display some similarities and shared characteristics with the English system. For example, state funding is the primary source of income for FECs in most of the countries examined, although the level of government investment varies considerably. Tri-partite collaborations between government, industry and education providers to determine qualifications and curricula are also common place; some countries, such as Canada, have taken collaboration to the next level, engaging businesses on a commercial level. Colleges are increasingly providing a diverse range of vocational options –particularly apprenticeships - as well as higher education and informal adult learning opportunities, in addition to their core offer. Community responsibility is now also high on the agenda for most countries. Incentives are often used to encourage learners to continue with their learning and persuade employers to provide support; however, too much government intervention can reduce the inclination and opportunity to pursue independent income streams for colleges. Finally, the present government in England is seeking to devolve greater powers to local communities, including colleges, to shape local policy. Decentralisation has been implemented in several other countries and resulted in greater local autonomy; however quality control and performance management are key factors in ensuring power is successfully devolved.

International comparisons with the English FEC system have identified some interesting issues. However, the considerable diversity in the political, economic and historical circumstances of each nation means that it is highly unlikely that one model could be easily transferred and applied in an English context. Moreover, international experience suggests that policy reforms may be more likely to succeed within systems that are stable and have a coherent long-term strategy, enabling consensus and trust to be built with key stakeholders over a long period of time. As we will demonstrate in the next chapter, the English system has evolved in a highly unstable environment and has been subject to constant change. This should be taken into account when drawing on the practice of other nations to inform the development of the domestic system.[95]

---

95 Hawley, J. (2006).

3 Policy context

Skills have long since been integral to government policy. However, the current recession has placed renewed emphasis on skills issues. The present government has introduced a number of changes designed to free up the FE sector to respond to the needs of the economy and help bring the country out of recession. These, and the implications for FECs, are considered in this chapter.

FECs have been operating in a dynamic policy context for many years, driven by political objectives to plug perceived gaps in the skills system and drive up productivity. Appendix 1 summarises the organisational and structural changes to the skills system that have been implemented since Labour took power in 1997. Whilst review and change can be a good thing, the rate at which policy has altered and the volume of initiatives that have emerged has left the FE sector in a constant state of flux and some employers simply unable to keep up.

Back in 2005, Foster set out a vision for a further education system focused on learner achievement and community impact.[96] His aim was to create an environment in which young people and adults could achieve their full potential, both personally and professionally, and in doing so, contribute to national prosperity and social cohesion. The key to this vision was the development of a coherent framework spanning schools as well as the further and higher education sectors. Within that framework, Foster advocated the development of a distinct and nationally *'recognised brand'* for the FE sector based on a *'shared core purpose'* focused on skills and employability.

In order for his vision to be fully realised, Foster argued that lessons from the strategic and management practices of other public sector services both at home and abroad should be learned and that investments in staff development and effective leadership were required. He also advocated the loosening of centralised controls and the implementation of a simplified inspection regime based on self

---

96   Foster, A (2005).

regulation and clear accountability structures for the sector. Learners were to be placed at the centre of the development of policy and practice, which emphasised the importance of collaboration and specialisation for increased learner choice and streamlined progression pathways underpinned by effective information, advice and guidance (IAG).

The government of the day welcomed many of Foster's recommendations, including the increased focus on FE's role in community development and the shift towards service-user orientated provision for both employers and individuals.[97] Their response was to re-focus policy objectives on tackling employers' operational skill needs and increase a sense of ownership amongst beneficiaries through initiatives such as the Individual Learner Account pilot. The call to better support minority groups such as learners with learning difficulties and/or disabilities (LLDD) was backed by a commitment to improve the quality and access to suitable provision through an investment programme. While these developments were largely welcomed by the sector, concerns were expressed that emerging policy overlooked the needs of the adult learning population.[98]

Twelve months on from Foster, the final report of the Leitch Review was published.[99] It recommended a series of challenging targets to improve productivity and growth in the UK as well as the nation's position in relation to its international competitors. Focused on the UK's long term skills needs, Leitch set a number of targets for 2020 including increasing the proportion of adults with basic skills and qualifications at Levels 2, 3 and 4, and boosting the number of Apprenticeships delivered each year. However, these targets and policies were based on an assumption that qualifications are an effective proxy for skills and that skills are the key driver of economic growth and prosperity; these assumptions have subsequently been shown to be flawed. Research published in 2009 demonstrates that although the qualifications gap between the UK and other countries has

97 DfES (2006).
98 NIACE (2005b).
99 Leitch, S. (2006).

narrowed, actual skill levels have remained largely unchanged.[100] Further work to boost skill levels is, therefore, required. However, skills acquisition is unlikely to solve the productivity gap; greater emphasis must also be placed on the effective deployment and utilisation of skills in the workplace.[101]

The current Coalition Government published its skills strategy, *Skills for Sustainable Growth* in November 2010, setting out significant reforms to adult learning and skills based upon the principles of fairness, responsibility and freedom.[102] The accompanying investment strategy *Investing in Skills for Sustainable Growth* sets out how the government intends to achieve its objectives through its investment in FE and skills.[103]

The current strategy takes a wider view of the FE system and acknowledges its role in promoting social inclusion and mobility, as well as skills. It also seeks to devolve greater powers to citizens, employers and communities to shape local skills policy and provision, targeting public resources at those who need them most, and placing greater responsibility on individuals and employers for ensuring their own skills needs are met, including contributing to the cost of learning. The intended outcomes of the reforms are increased productivity and employment, (particularly within skilled professions that generate high economic value), and a reduction in both skills deficiencies and the number of 19-24 year olds who are not in education, employment or training (NEET).

The skills strategy is located within an over-arching framework of reforms, which has been shaped by the recession and the imperatives to reduce the national debt and stimulate growth. This agenda presents both opportunities and challenges to the public sector as a whole which must respond within the constraints of reduced budgets. The reforms are also set within the context of the 'Big Society' agenda which invokes a new notion of collective local leadership. Two of the Big Society themes are particularly pertinent to colleges and echo Foster's earlier focus on the importance of the community: first, to

---

100 Shury, J. (2010).
101 Centre for Enterprise (2007).
102 BIS (2010e).
103 BIS (2010a).

"give communities more powers", and second to *"encourage people to take an active role in their communities"* to improve their own lives and the lives of those around them.[104] These themes have implications both for the ways in which colleges respond as learning providers, and for the contribution that colleges make to the communities within which they are situated. FECs have an integral role to play but as research by LSIS suggests, this will involve extending the reach of traditional college leadership beyond the institutional setting into the communities they serve.[105]

Funding

In April 2010, the Skills Funding Agency assumed responsibility for funding and regulating adult further education and skills training in England as well as overseeing the implementation of significant changes to the FE funding system. Driven by fiscal restraints and the ambition to increase the level of individual contribution to the cost of learning, the FE resources budget will be reduced by 25 per cent by 2014-15 and capital funding will also be reduced during the same period. However, a new Growth and Innovation Fund of £50m per year has been created to encourage employers to raise skill levels and grow their businesses. Support from the Union Learning Fund and use of the European Social Fund will also continue. Since April 2011, public funding for FE adult education provision (including Apprenticeships) has been administered from a single Adult Skills Budget, replacing the Adult Learner Responsive and Employer Responsive funds.

The changes to FE funding have been accompanied by a rationalisation in data collection, a reduction in regulatory requirements and a commitment to abolish top-down skills targets for providers. The overall aim of the reforms is to reduce bureaucracy and allow greater flexibility, innovation and responsiveness at the local level.

---

104 Cabinet Office (2010).
105 LSIS (2010d).

From spring 2010, new arrangements were also put in place to fund qualifications and individual units on the Qualifications and Credit Framework (QCF). A series of trials are currently underway to establish the extent to which funding at the unit level will enable providers to realise the flexibilities within the QCF.[106] The aim is to support and encourage those learners who otherwise would not engage in learning to work towards a qualification by accumulating credits in bite-sized chunks. Although unitisation has been broadly welcomed by training organisations, it presents challenges for many who still need support to interpret data and clarify their offers to respective learner groups (e.g. unemployed and employed). There are also concerns that some aspects of delivery still need to be worked through and uncertainties around what this will mean in practice.

Priority groups and entitlements

Public funding for FE adult education provision will be more closely focused on key target groups and aligned with policy priorities designed to move individuals into employment. A new set of entitlements, fee remissions and limits will be introduced over the next three years; individuals and employers who fall outside of the priority groups will be expected to bear a greater proportion of the costs of training themselves. In summary, adult funding is predominantly targeted at the following groups:

Apprenticeships

Apprenticeship numbers are forecast to increase by at least 250,000. In response, funding for Adult Apprenticeships will increase by up to £250m during the current Spending Review period. Adult Apprenticeships (Level 2) will remain co-funded at 50% and learners will be able to access loans for Advanced Apprenticeships (Level 3). Providers will also be expected to give due consideration to the development of clear progression routes from Apprenticeships to higher level training.

---

106 Skills Funding Agency (2011).

Basic Skills

Adult basic skills remain a priority. The government will provide full funding for literacy and numeracy provision from entry level up to and including Level 2. Despite this, the priority funding rate uplift for some Skills for Life provision will be removed, meaning that the unit of funding per basic skills learner will be reduced. English for Speakers of Other Languages (ESOL) will also be fully funded if the learner is looking for work; however, there will be no public funding available for those accessing workplace training, and non-work based training will be co-funded by individuals. In short, publicly-funded ESOL provision will be prioritised for those whose lack of English is preventing them from entering the labour market.

The unemployed

Funding eligibility criteria are specifically focused on moving individuals into employment. The government will fully fund targeted training for those claiming 'active' benefits to help them address any skills gaps which are acting as a barrier to re-entering work. New Job Outcome Incentive Payments will act as an incentive for FECs and training providers to offer training that can result in a job. The government will also invest in training for offenders to help get them into work and reduce the likelihood of reoffending. Further flexibilities have also been announced allowing providers to offer fully subsidised courses to some learners on a wider range of benefits if the training is designed to help them move into employment.[107]

Learners with Learning Difficulties and/or Disabilities

LLDDs will continue to have the same entitlements and access to provision as other groups. The government expects providers to recognise the needs of these groups when planning delivery.

The response of the FE sector to the funding prioritisation reforms has been mixed and is highly dependent on the nature of the organi-

107 BIS (2011).

sation (e.g. size and specialism) and their offer to learners. What is apparent, nonetheless, is that representatives from the FE sector broadly welcome the increased emphasis on greater learner choice and communicated freedoms in adult budget administration.

> "Adult further education learners should be able to make their own choices, and in order to do this, colleges must be given the rights to manage fee policies, as higher education institutions do. We fully support the coalition government's five principals, as outlined in its recent white paper, and hope that this policy direction will lead to a fairer entitlement for adults in further education colleges."[108]
>
> Frank McLoughlin CBE, Chair of the 157 Group

Co-investment

Going forward, greater emphasis will be placed on 'co-investment' and the need for learners and employers to take responsibility for their own learning and development.[109] Research previously undertaken by the Institute for Employment Studies and NIACE suggests that this position is broadly supported: *"A survey of adults found that the majority felt that the individual and the employer, rather than the taxpayer, should bear most of the funding."*[110] However, the risk that demand could be reduced because some individuals will not be able or prepared to pay is also recognised. Participation amongst the next generation of learners who may be required to take out loans for both their further and higher education must be closely monitored in order to establish whether cost does act as a disincentive for engagement.

The argument that employers *should* co-invest in skills development may be hard to make, particularly in difficult economic times, as research by the Work Foundation found that *"there is little concrete evidence from Britain that employers' investment in training*

---

108 157 Group (2011a).
109 Banks, C. N. (2010).
110 Hillage, J., Uden, T., Aldridge, F. and Eccles, J. (2000).

produces a financial return".[111] The picture is further complicated when the question of engagement with small and medium sized enterprises (SMEs) is considered, as their needs may be more diverse and less clearly articulated than larger businesses. In SMEs, it is often the learner that acts as the point of contact and mediates between the skills provider and employer.[112]

The reforms present opportunities to re-plan budget allocation and utilise funding in a more creative way to ensure that priority learners in their catchment areas continue to be supported and access relevant training. There are, however, risks surrounding the exclusion of certain hard to reach groups who may not be able to invest in training or take on loans. Fee remissions in areas such as ESOL will have a large impact on colleges located in areas with high numbers of non English speaking communities. It is uncertain to what extent such groups, who may be most in need of access to training for their livelihood, could be disadvantaged.

Minimum contract levels

The government is also proposing to introduce minimum contract values of £500,000 from 2011. However, this will have serious implications for smaller providers currently delivering contracts valued at less than this as there is a risk that these providers will lose their public funding and could go out of business. The HayGroup suggest that mergers and/or acquisitions could help overcome the challenges faced by smaller, individual institutions. They argue that new 'mega-colleges' would be better placed to contribute to the 'Big Society' agenda as they would have stronger local engagement with their communities and a wide range of partners to work with. It has been suggested that larger colleges may, as a result of their management structures, also be better placed to exploit new collaborative opportunities.[113] Whilst it is true that these arrangements could help to

---

111 Hillage, J., Uden, T., Aldridge, F. and Eccles, J. (2000).
112 Kelly, S. (2007a).
113 KPMG (2010).

tackle regional need through the provision of a high volume of places and diverse networks, there is also the possibility that some of the local, highly responsive and specialist tailored provision may be lost. Indeed, John Hayes, in his speech on the current vision for FE, cautioned against the widespread merger and acquisition of colleges. In his view, a smaller number of large organisations is not the solution to failing colleges; in order to achieve a *"revitalised and dynamic system"* a wider range of approaches needs to be developed, including innovation, collaboration and partnership.[114]

Although there is evidence throughout this report that many FECs are already working with a range of organisations, the prevailing culture of competition between providers could act as a barrier to collaboration and partnership working between them.[115] Research by KPMG suggests that this barrier is not simply based on the legal or regulatory framework but rather that the competitive model has become entrenched within the sector.[116] Ways of overcoming this barrier will need to be developed. However, if it can be overcome, colleges would be free to develop alliances with higher education, schools and other training providers *"to form new ecologies of local adult and lifelong learning"*.[117]

Within a straitened funding regime, colleges are likely to seek to both minimise expenditure as well as increase income. In *Doing more for less,* the 157 Group outline the innovative ways in which colleges in the UK and overseas are responding to the current challenges and increasing revenues including: adopting innovative, flexible and responsive commercial models; expanding training and learning for business and industry; differentiating products and services; and developing new pricing models as well as working in partnership.[118] In order to minimise expenditure, opportunities to share back office services could be further exploited, with research suggesting that the services of a neutral third party facilitator aids success in this area.[119]

---

114 Hayes, J. (2011).
115 Collinson, D. (ed.) (2007).
116 KPMG (2010).
117 Howard, U. (2009).
118 157 Group (2011).
119 KPMG (2010).

Collaboration in the provision of frontline services is more complex, and likely to become more so as the recommendations of the Wolf Report on vocational education are implemented.[120] A number of models for collaboration, such as setting up standalone companies (including social enterprises and community interest companies), entering into joint ventures, and acquiring companies, are extant, although questions remain as to whether all colleges are confident that they possess the skills necessary to take these options forward. Also within the sector, there appears to be an appetite for exploring the possible benefits of a mutual model that utilises high staff engagement to drive innovation and change while maintaining a sense of public service at its heart; however these developments are at an early stage.[121]

Summary

One of the most notable features of the English FE system over the past 10 years is the continuous change to policy and the associated priorities for the sector. The only constant has been the focus on the acquisition of skills through qualifications. This lack of stability and the complexity in the system that it engenders has had serious implications for colleges and the way in which they engage with wider stakeholders, such as employers. The latest skills strategy takes a wider view of the FE system and takes account of the important role that colleges play in promoting and supporting social inclusion and mobility. Although the delivery of skills remains a key priority, this does represent a slight departure from this historical policy stance.

Despite international evidence to suggest that policy reforms may be more likely to succeed within systems that are stable and have a coherent long-term strategy, further reforms to the FE system will be phased in over the next three years. Funding will be much more closely aligned with employment outcomes and targeted at those that are furthest from the labour market. Individuals and employers will be expected to co-fund many qualifications. However, in the current

120 Wolf, A. (2011).
121 Vocademix (2011).

economic climate, the argument that employers *should* co-invest in skills development may be hard to make. In addition, concerns have been raised that the new arrangements could have a negative impact on take-up and progression, especially amongst disadvantaged groups, which would represent a retrograde step in the battle to widen participation and increase access.

The introduction of minimum contract levels appears to be at odds with the desire to increase competition by encouraging new entrants, including third sector organisations and small private training providers, into the market place; it is also expected to have a disproportionate effect on those smaller training providers that are already operating within the system as some will be unlikely to meet the threshold for direct funding from the Skills Funding Agency. Developing relationships with bigger providers such as colleges or large training providers may be the key to their survival. Although this presents opportunities for greater efficiencies and increased economies of scale, there is a risk that specialist, tailored provision could be lost. In addition, the prevailing culture of competition between providers will need to be challenged in order to make genuine collaboration and partnership working between providers a reality.

4 Identifying the needs of communities

FECs have a long track record of working with their communities in order to identify need and help shape local skills policy. They engage with a complex network of partnerships at a strategic level, as well as with individual organisations and learners.

This chapter explores college links with partnership organisations and the public, private and voluntary sector, as well as their use of Labour Market Intelligence when shaping and developing local skills policy. It also considers the ways in which FECs engage with learners and employers in order to identify their specific learning requirements.

Local skills planning

Colleges have played a vital role in the employment and skills system over a number of years. This has involved engagement with a range of organisations within and outside the education sector (including private businesses and employer representative bodies) and membership of partnerships such as: Local Strategic Partnerships and Employment and Skills Boards. The current skills strategy of the Coalition Government continues to stress the importance of collaboration and consultation between colleges and employer-led boards, as well as local authorities and Jobcentre Plus. The aim is to ensure that colleges understand the needs of their communities and develop an appreciation of local skills issues so that they can embed local priorities within their business plans and strategies.[122]

---

122 CFE (2009b).

In light of the abolition of regional development agencies, the skills strategy also highlights the importance of college engagement with the emerging Local Enterprise Partnerships (LEP). There is an expectation that colleges will share their plans with LEPs to ensure *"alignment between the economic development priorities and the skills provision available locally"*.[123] However, a small study into the role of LEPs in tackling skills needs suggests that attempting to align college plans with those of the LEP could create a number of tensions.[124] For example, LEPs are focused on increasing the number of qualifications at Level 3 and above whilst colleges represent students studying at all levels. In addition, LEPs are organised geographically, whereas many colleges, such as specialist national providers, are not. Ensuring college plans that span geographical boundaries are aligned with the priorities of one or more LEPs presents a key challenge.

The recent House of Commons Inquiry recommended that further education involvement in LEPs was *"particularly important to addressing skills gaps...LEPs should consider co-opting representatives of further education and higher education onto their governing bodies, either permanently or on an ad hoc basis"*.[125] As key partners involved in both shaping and delivering skills at the local level, colleges are encouraged to take a pro-active stance: *"they should not wait to be asked, but should take the initiative and make the case that their contribution is essential."*[126] However, recent research highlighted concerns regarding the extent to which LEPs would effectively engage with providers.[127] The study suggests that, in practice, it will not be feasible for all providers to be represented on the LEP; rather, it was agreed that providers should be involved in developing LEP policies at a second tier level.

In addition to their main business as learning providers, colleges have typically contributed towards the achievement of wider local

---

123 BIS (2010e, p.54).
124 Davis, P. (2011).
125 House of Commons Business, Innovation and Skills Committee (2010).
126 LSIS (2010c, p. 11).
127 Davis, P. (2011).

economic and social objectives such as developing community cohesion, tackling unemployment, re-integrating offenders, promoting active citizenship and tackling social isolation. They have also played a vital role in social and economic planning for many years through their involvement with a wide range of organisations including: the voluntary and community sector; local businesses and employer representative bodies; the Police; NHS; and schools and other learning providers; as well as their membership of partnerships such as Local Area Agreement sub-groups and town centre and regeneration partnerships.[128, 129] Engagement with these partnerships and organisations, alongside learners and employers, provides the mechanisms through which colleges can *"create a better understanding of their communities and citizens"*, enabling them to respond effectively.[130]

This broader role for colleges in their communities was mandated in law in 2009 when the Apprenticeships, Skills, Children and Learning Act placed a duty on colleges to promote economic and social well-being in their local area through *"consulting, seeking advice or assistance from, providing advice or assistance to, or collaborating or otherwise participating in joint working with, other educational institutions, employers or other persons (who may be, or include, persons outside the local area)"*.[131] Through this work providers are able to identify not only skills needs but wider social needs of their communities which the college may be able to meet either through courses or the wider work they carry out.

The role of partnership working in local social and economic planning is therefore key. A recent report by NFER which examined partnership work between colleges, local authorities and LSPs highlighted a number of key lessons for effective collaboration.[132] These include:

- creating a relationship based on trust, respect, openness, honesty and transparency;
- having confidence in the other partners to deliver;

---

128 CFE (2009b).
129 CFE (2011).
130 LSIS (2010c, p. 10).
131 Great Britain Parliament (2009).
132 McCrone, T., Southcott, C. and Evans, K. (2009).

- shared understanding and belief in the work, including a shared vision with clear roles, responsibilities and decision making processes;
- regular and robust communication systems; and
- the involvement of key senior/strategic leaders.

Research suggests that ensuring sufficient time and resources are dedicated to partnership activities is also vital, along with a recognition that partners operate in different ways and that competing priorities can impact on the speed at which organisations can act.[133,134, 135] Given that time and resources are limited, developing a detailed understanding of all the different partnerships, and deciding which ones to become involved with, poses a further challenge for some colleges.

Identifying the needs of individual learners

As noted previously, FECs serve a wide range of adult learners who have different needs. Colleges have been highly attuned to the distinct characteristics and needs of adult learners throughout their existence. Alan Tuckett observes in his thematic paper commissioned as part of the Foster Review, that *"adults learn part-time, often episodically, occasionally on day release or in other intensive spells, and for a diversity of purposes."*[136] As a result, both the content and processes of adult learning require a different approach to that employed for younger learners. However, it is important to recognise that adults may not perceive their learning experience as episodic, instead regarding it as a single coherent journey.[137] Therefore, a key ongoing challenge for colleges is to provide a seamless learning experience that recognises and takes account of the episodic and varying nature of adult education.

The rich array of individuals who choose to return to learning in a college environment bring a wealth of prior knowledge, skills and

133   LSIS (2010c).
134   CFE (2009).
135   McCrone, T., Southcott, C. and Evans, K. (2009).
136, 137 Tuckett, A. (2005).

experience.[138] Research suggests that colleges should develop mechanisms to exploit this resource more effectively as there are considerable benefits to involving learners in the development of their own education and the organisations in which they study.[139]

Numerous typologies have emerged which seek to define both the level and type of organisational engagement with learners and the wider community. An example of one that draws on a range of work in this field is provided in Appendix 2.[140] This model categorises learning providers according to their activities and places them on a continuum which ranges from institution-led at one extreme to student-led at the other. Colleges that are located towards the 'student-led' end of this continuum are utilising a variety of mechanisms to capture the 'learner voice' in their institutions. These include the use of familiar methods of engagement such as: learner surveys; suggestion boxes; documented complaints procedures; 'have your say days';[141] learner conferences;[142] student governors and student councils.[143, 144] Providers that have further embedded the learner voice into their practices have: instituted meetings between student representatives and the Senior Leadership Team; introduced Principal's Question Time; involved students in policy and strategy reviews as well as in grading provision against the Common Inspection Framework; and/or engaged students in observations to monitor teacher performance and involved them in recruitment panels for teaching staff.[145, 146]

Approaches that place the learner voice at the heart of curriculum and organisational development have shown to have a positive impact on the student learning experience which in turn helps to raise learners' aspirations; encourage learners to take a higher degree of responsibility for their own learning; and increase learner motivation, engagement,

---

138 Collinson, D. (2007)
139 Evans, L. (2005).
140 Rudd, T., Colligan, F. and Naik, R. (2006).
141 Forrest, C., Lawton, J., Adams, A., Louth, T. and Swain, I. (2007).
142 Shuttle, J. (2007).
143 Fielding, M. (2006).
144 LSIS (2009b).
145 Fielding, M. (2006).
146 LSIS (2009b).

achievement and progression. It also ensures issues relating to teaching and learning, pastoral support or enrichment are swiftly resolved.[147, 148] It can also support self-assessment, continuous quality improvement and sustainable organisational change which can have wider benefits for learners, learning providers and the wider community.[149]

The success of these initiatives is attributed to a range of factors. Literature suggests that the appointment of learner engagement champions, such as Student Liaison Officers, can help to increase learner engagement by raising the profile of the learner voice, empowering learners to make their voices heard, and developing new ways of engaging learners and wider communities.[150] They also help to create trusting relationships between learners and educators, which is paramount for effective engagement. With trust comes the perception that learners are valued within the institution; they are free to express their opinions and concerns, and actively encouraged to take ownership for the contributions they make to decision-making processes.[151] In order to further engender this level of trust, there is evidence that some colleges have implemented buddying, mentoring and coaching schemes.[152]

Other factors crucial to the successful integration of the learner voice within colleges are: the level of organisational buy-in to the concept of the 'learner voice' and the extent to which it is integrated across all aspects of the institution;[153] the extent to which staff are prepared to challenge existing practices and to be challenged;[154, 155] the level of support for out-reach activities;[156, 157] and the prevalence of student-led leadership models.[158] The importance of organisational buy-in

147 Forrest, C., Lawton, J., Adams, A., Louth, T. and Swain, I. (2007).
148 Collinson, D. (2007).
149 Forrest, C., Lawton, J., Adams, A., Louth, T. and Swain, I. (2007).
150 LSIS (2009c).
151 Shuttle, J. (2007).
152 Fielding, M. (2006).
153 Shuttle, J. (2007).
154 Forrest, C., Lawton, J., Adams, A., Louth, T. and Swain, I. (2007).
155 LSIS (2009c).
156 Gallacher, J., Mayes, T. and Crossan, B. (2007).
157 Hannon, P., Pahl, K., Bird, V., Taylor, C. and Birch, C. (2003).
158 Shuttle, J. (2007).

and the innovative use of technology to capture student views are detailed in the case study of Northampton College.[159, 160, 161]

Learner engagement, Northampton College, Northampton, UK

Northampton College has used a variety of methods to engage with its learners and ensure that their voice is heard. In 2009 Barry Hansford, the College's Head of Learner Support, won the LSIS Leadership and Learner Voice award for Principal or Senior Leader of the Year. As the result of launching a Learner Involvement Strategy in mid 2007 and encouraging key members of staff to provide learners with clear information and guidance, a whole host of activities to refresh existing and establish new learner engagement methods took place. These activities included: learner forums to discuss issues related to teaching and learning as well as college-wide issues; a series of learner focused events including an annual learner conference to inform the quality improvement process; an annual learner voice week; Principal's question time; and recruiting student governors to represent learners' views to the college's senior management and work alongside the student union to develop the learner experience. Barry's support in helping students to organise these activities resulted in much greater level of student involvement. Mark Owen, the college's learner support manager, commented:

"As a result, communication between staff and students has reached an all time high and a real feeling of togetherness has developed. Learners' needs are at the heart of everything we do, and the information gained from them has become part of our decision-making process."

In addition to these more traditional learner engagement methods, the college has also been praised for its innovative use of technology to gather students' views and stimulate feedback. Such innovations have included:

- the use of 'Who Wants to be a Millionaire' style voting pads to gather student feedback at the learner conference;
- a 'Big Brother' style diary room for learners to record their views at the learner conference;
- using video camcorders to capture sound bites from learners regarding their thoughts on lessons and other topics, which was used to develop an in-house TV programme broadcast in the college;

159 LSIS (2009b).
160 LSIS (2010b).
161 Northampton College (2010).

- SMS text messaging, whereby students are encouraged to text a 5 digit number to share their views on their learning experience and any new ideas for events, in addition to the college using texts to liaise with students;
- email buttons in the college's Virtual Learning Environment, whereby learners can submit their feedback to the senior management team at the click of a button with a 24 hour response time;
- online surveys and the use of iPads to capture real-time feedback during enrolment week and throughout the year; and
- electronic Individual Learning Plans to facilitate the exchange of information, including topics such as attendance, progress, support and discipline.

Barry Hansford highlighted:

"Becoming more innovative with how we engage with learners and use their opinions and ideas to make real change was always the main driver. Technology is a means to an end – we know that learners, in particular our younger learners, use technology intuitively. We now have a range of simple

The process of integrating the learner voice is not, however, without its challenges. In order to be effective, the learner voice must be representative of all of the college's communities; the learners who are chosen to share their views must, therefore, represent the wider constituency.[162] Research demonstrates that many of the more common practices for capturing the learner voice implemented by FECs are campus-based. Although they are very effective at engaging full-time learners who attend college on a regular basis, levels of engagement with those who are studying part-time or at a distance, such as work-based learners and those located at outreach centres, are poor.[163]

Despite this, evidence suggests that some providers are placing a particular emphasis on engaging with hard to reach and under-represented groups within their local communities, in order to tackle some of the wider issues that can act as a barrier to learning, such as disability, bullying, hate crime, refugees and asylum seekers, and Young Officials support widening participation objectives.[164] There are

162 Forrest, C., Lawton, J., Adams, A., Louth, T. and Swain, I. (2007).
163 Katsifli, D. and Green, K. (2010).
164 LSIS (2009b).

examples of colleges that have consulted with Black and Minority Ethnic Groups and Faith Groups to uncover the barriers they experience to participation in FE. This has led to developing more effective strategies and initiatives to increase participation and bridge the attainment gap. These include community-based ESOL courses[165] and pastoral support for students, families and staff to help deal with difficult situations which have cultural or religious implications, such as forced marriages and the wearing of religious symbols.[166] However, as we noted in Chapter 3, changes in entitlements for ESOL provision could put some of this work under threat.

In order to contribute their views in an effective and appropriate manner, research suggests that learners need to be able to both reflect on their learning experience and articulate their feelings.[167] Not all students will be equipped with the skills to do this. In particular, those who represent marginalised communities may need additional support and encouragement to take on the role.

Identifying employer need

Colleges have been engaging with employers, either directly or indirectly, for some time, encouraged by successive government White papers on skills and reports such as Leitch and Foster.[168] Employers have a significant role to play in both articulating skills needs (demand) and shaping provision (supply).

Employers have a vested interest in ensuring that the skills system is fit for purpose. Their involvement with the system is primarily driven by economic imperatives to remain competitive and increase productivity[169] through the creation of a flexible and highly skilled workforce.[170, 171] There is evidence that employers have been involved

165 Collinson, M. and Collinson, D. (2007).
166 LSIS (2009b).
167 Forrest, C., Lawton, J., Adams, A., Louth, T. and Swain, I. (2007).
168 Collinson, M. and Collinson, D. (2008).
169 UKCES (2010).
170 Kelly, S. (2007).
171 CBI (2009).

in shaping and influencing priorities and provision for many years.[172, 73] For example, in the 1980s, employers were actively engaged with sectoral bodies to define occupational standards for National Vocational Qualifications (NVQs); more recently employers were represented on the partnerships charged with the development of the 14-19 Diplomas.[174] Employers have traditionally engaged with the skills system in a variety of ways including: *"articulating skills needs, supporting policy development, influencing government spend and priorities on training, influencing training content, providing feedback on training or system improvement, and increasing their own and other employers' investment in training".*[175] As a result, the concept of the 'employer voice' in skills policy is, therefore, multi-faceted and often interpreted differently by different partnerships and organisations. There is evidence that this has led to confusion regarding the role of business and disillusionment amongst some employers who feel their views have not been listened to and/or acted upon.

The differing roles employers fulfil in relation to different aspects of the skills system can be characterised in one of three ways:[176]

- Employer-involved – where the opinions and views of employers are sought but employers are not responsible for decision-making.
- Shared responsibility – where employers and other organisations share decision making.
- Employer-led – where employers are completely responsible for the decisions which are made.

However, as the model in Appendix 3 demonstrates, even *within* the myriad of bodies which have been established to shape the skills system along spatial and/or sectoral lines, employers assume different roles and possess varying degrees of responsibility, depending on the issues under consideration. The situation is further complicated because businesses are often involved in multiple partnerships which

---

172   UKCES (2010).
173   Kelly, S. (2007b).
174   Erlt, H and Statsz, C. (2010).
175, 176   UKCES (2010).

also accord them different roles and responsibilities. Despite the current rhetoric surrounding the development of an employer-*led* system, the evidence suggests that current mechanisms for engagement are predominantly employer-*involved*.

Outside of direct marketing activities, evidence suggests that colleges engage with employers through a variety of other activities such as employer forums.[177] Appendix 4 outlines a range of employer engagement activities which providers take part in. These provide opportunities for colleges to interact with business in order to develop a better understanding of local need and include: curriculum development; college governance; and the development and delivery of bespoke training.[178]

Direct engagement with individual employers is often supplemented with management information including Labour Market Intelligence (LMI)[179] and market research with employers at a local and sector level.[180] Recent research has found that colleges are using LMI to aid their planning processes; however they are more likely to use localised contextual data sourced directly rather than using national LMI which focuses on national skills priorities.[181] This information is then used to inform the college's business plan, course portfolio and teaching strategy. Although it is recognised that this high level aggregated data can be less useful when developing specific provision with individual employers, it does indicate the broad skill areas which may need to be addressed in the future within the communities they serve. Research outlined in the recent UKCES publication also found that local labour market surveys are useful at the national or sectoral level, but not at a local authority level or below.[182] Alongside this, there is a concern that there could be future gaps in labour market data collection as a result of the abolition of the Regional Development Agencies; it is, as yet, unclear as to whether the LEPs will take up this role.

---

177   LSN (2010).
178   Macleod, D. and Hughes, M (2005.
179, 180 Ofsted (2004a).
181   CFE (2011).
182   UKCES (2011).

Summary

Colleges have been a vital part of the skills system for many years and have been working in partnership with a range of organisations in both the public and private sectors to identify the social as well as economic needs of their communities. Partnership work has been integral to ensuring colleges are both responsive and accountable to their local communities, and fulfil a central role in shaping local social and economic plans. It is likely that partnership working will continue to be an integral element of any strategy moving forwards. However, given the myriad of partnerships and the limited time and resources available to engage with them, deciding which ones to become involved with will present a key challenge for some colleges.

Moving forward, colleges will have an important role to play within LEPs, helping to identify and address skills gaps and shortages. However, engagement with LEPs will not be without its challenges. Differences in geographical reach and conflicting priorities could act as a barrier to engagement. However, early indications suggest there is agreement within the sector that colleges should actively seek to influence policies set by LEPs. Given it is not possible for every college to be represented on a LEP, effective mechanisms need to be developed to ensure the collective view of providers in the LEP footprint is taken into account and contributes to shaping local leadership.

Greater devolution presents an opportunity for providers to set their own priorities in response to local need. Engaging with communities to shape and articulate strategic priorities and the curriculum will be essential if providers are to be judged as both responsive and accountable to their local communities.

There are numerous examples of colleges that are already successfully integrating the learner voice into organisational developments, including changes to systems and processes, learner support, and the curriculum. However, more needs to be done to ensure the views of all learner communities, including work-based and part-time students, are represented. In addition, further investigation into how existing good practice can be adopted in community settings is required; in particular, how the most disenfranchised can be empowered to 'have their say' and take full advantage of provision that is targeted specifically at them.

Colleges also use a range of mechanisms to engage with and identify the needs of employers in the communities they serve. However, the evidence suggests that there is still some distance to go before the system could be described as truly employer-*led*. In the context of a demand-led system, the 'employer voice' will continue to be important in ensuring colleges both effectively identify need as well as develop appropriate provision to meet that need. The development of effective employer engagement strategies is, therefore, likely to remain, if not increase in importance in the coming years.

5 Meeting the needs of communities

Colleges meet the needs of their various communities through supporting learners, tailoring provision for different learning communities and working in partnership.

This section explores how colleges meet the needs of their different communities. It outlines the ways in which colleges support learners and contribute to widening participation through outreach work, IAG, and the use of information and communication technology (ICT). It also examines the partnership work that colleges are involved in to meet the needs of employers. The section concludes by considering the current challenges for colleges in meeting the needs of their communities as well as the potential opportunities and solutions.

What colleges do

First and foremost, colleges are institutions of further education, established to deliver learning and skills to young people and adults. FECs have developed a number of approaches to delivery, in addition to their full-time campus-based offer, designed to meet the wide-ranging learning and support needs of students and widen participation objectives. Much provision is, therefore, delivered on a part-time basis, and in a variety of physical and virtual settings, which ensures it is as accessible as possible to all, irrespective of individual circumstances and/or preferred learning styles. Some of these approaches are explored below.

Community learning

Evidence suggests that colleges undertake outreach work to help tackle social exclusion and enable individuals, who would otherwise find it difficult to engage in learning in a FEC, to study in their local community.[183]

Outreach work is, therefore, designed to help individuals overcome barriers to learning and ensure they are supported to stay on their course.[184] For many, often disadvantaged groups, outreach provides a stepping stone back into learning and offers a second chance to develop valuable skills.[185]

Many colleges have implemented community-based initiatives designed to facilitate better access to groups that are typically marginalised within a local area.[186, 187] These include establishing Community Learning Centres (CLCs)[188] and appointing Education Community Link Workers.[189] Providing services in the community offers a flexible solution that ensures learning can be delivered at a time and location that is both convenient and familiar for the learner. The informality of these settings allows the learner to bring significant aspects of their personal and social lives with them into the learning environment, which they may find difficult to do in a formal setting.[190] Both of these features help to overcome key barriers to participation; in addition, new learning centres can also support the achievement of wider community objectives such as the economic regeneration of an area.[191]

The use of ICT

Technology is increasingly fulfilling a key role in the delivery of numerous aspects of the curriculum both on and off campus. Its main strength is its flexibility: technology is not bound by space and time and can facilitate access to learning for groups that otherwise would find it difficult to engage, such as those based in rural locations, those who are housebound, or those who need to fit learning around other commitments including work or family.[192] Technology allows learners to be *"virtually off-site without being physically off-site, either through*

183	Policy Research Institute (2007).
184	Collinson, M. and Collinson, D. (2005).
185	157 Group (2010).
186	Hannon, P., Pahl, K., Bird, V., Taylor, C. and Birch, C. (2003).
187, 188	Gallacher, J., Mayes, T. and Crossan, B. (2007).
189	Hannon, P., Pahl, K., Bird, V., Taylor, C. and Birch, C. (2003.
190	Gallacher, J., Mayes, T. and Crossan, B. (2007).
191	Forde, C. (2000).
192	DIUS (2008).

the auspices of the formal education institution or otherwise".[193]

Colleges are increasingly developing their technology infrastructure, with even small colleges deploying the use of VLEs (virtual learning environments). The most widely used learning platform is Moodle, followed by Blackboard/WebCT.[194] According to recent research, activities for which more than half of teaching staff use technology include: communicating with staff; planning lessons and creating resources; delivering lessons; uploading and storing digital resources; communicating with learners; and accessing management information. A key benefit of using technology for teaching staff is a reduction in the amount of time spent on these activities.[195]

Technology is changing with way students and teachers communicate and it is becoming increasingly *"fluid and multi-layered"*. According to Howell, an important element of this multi-layered interaction is computer-mediated communication (CMC). Teachers increasingly provide online modules and learning materials on departmental web pages, enabling students to participate in various 'technology-enhanced learning activities'.[196] In addition, students use CMC to support their studies and homework using resources such as Wikipedia, blogs, wikis, Youtube, Podcasting, Flickr, and Del.icio.us. Online forums, chat rooms and other social networking sites such as Facebook and MySpace also fulfil a key role and help to pass *"the content parcel around"*.[197]

New models of learning that utilise ICT emphasise *"collaborative and active learning rather than passive reception and absorption"*.[198] These approaches may help to engage learners *"alienated from structured education"*,[199] especially young people. In addition, growth in the use of the internet has increasingly led to the construction of knowledge *outside* the boundaries of traditional institutions. As a result, power within the learning relationship has shifted from the teacher as imparter of knowledge, to a situation in which learner and teacher take collaborative responsibility for learning and knowledge

193   Mauger, S. (2009).
194, 195 Becta (2010).
196   Howell, C. (2008).
197, 198 Mauger, S. (2009).
199   Tuckett, A. (2005).

creation.[200] It is argued that within this context, the learning process should be reconceptualised. A number of alternative models exist, including the rhizomatic model of Deleuze and Guattari advocated by Cormier.[201] The rhizomatic model is characterised by a network of semi-independent 'nodes' of activity, in which learners engage with one another, rather than with a single teacher at the centre, to collaborate and build knowledge:

> "In the rhizomatic model of learning, curriculum is not driven by pre-defined inputs from experts; it is constructed and negotiated in real time by the contributions of those engaged in the learning process."[202]

Learner support

Overcoming barriers and engaging individuals in learning is, however, only the first step on the journey. Many learners need personal and other support to remain engaged and successfully complete their programme. Outstanding learner support is perceived to be a key indicator of a successful college.[203] This could include financial assistance with transport or childcare costs, or help to overcome a disability or learning difficulty such as dyslexia. Irrespective of the nature of the support provided, it is most effective when the student is treated as an individual and the support is tailored to their particular needs. Importantly, the support must be instituted from the outset and be on-going throughout the learning experience.

In an environment where individuals and/or employers are required to co-invest in learning, the onus will be on colleges to provide public information, advice and guidance so that learners can make informed decisions about what and where to study. Tuckett argues that effective information, advice and guidance (IAG), both prior to and during learning, has a substantial impact on the retention of learners, and

200   Mauger, S. (2009).
201, 202   Cormier, D. (2008).
203   Ofsted (2004c).

their assessment of the value of that learning.[204] *Skills for Sustainable Growth* proposes that a comprehensive range of public information on learning opportunities should be gathered and disseminated via the National Careers Service website as well as the websites of learning providers.[205] However, this approach assumes that all learners are motivated to seek out and interrogate this information, and have the capabilities to do so.[206] This is not the case. Serious concerns have been raised about the erosion of careers education and guidance for young people in particular, and the implications poor decision-making could have for recruitment, retention and achievement in the FE sector.[207]

Evidence suggests there are numerous other sources of information and advice for potential learners. Workplace trainers and employers are a common source of advice,[208] along with union learning representatives, described as a *"proven resource for championing learning"*.[209] In response to the 2008 consultation by the Department for Innovation, Universities and Skills (DIUS) into Informal Adult Learning, Sheffield City Council suggest that advice and guidance provided by mentors or learning champions offers demonstrable benefits for the least confident learners who may find it difficult to access support from other sources.[210] Furthermore, *Skills for Sustainable Growth* proposes that providers work with Jobcentre Plus to identify appropriate training for individuals.[211] It has also been suggested that probation officers, health visitors, and the Citizens' Advice Bureau amongst others are valuable partners and could help to inform individuals about the nature and scope of the college offer.[212]

According to Howard, in a complex system like FE, encouraging simplicity in the methods of engagement with individuals and employers is key. She suggests that *"the development of a single portal for adult and lifelong learning in a locality"* would help to facilitate this

---

204   Tuckett, A. (2005).
205   BIS (2010e).
206   Mauger, S. (2009).
207   Hooley, T. and Watts, A. G. (2011).
208   Hillage, J., Uden, T., Aldridge, F. and Eccles, J. (2000).
209, 210 DIUS (2008).
211   BIS (2010e).
212   Schuller, T. and Watson, D. (2009).

process.[213] Although a single portal has yet to be established, technology is now used in many colleges to provide careers IAG.[214] For example, web-enabled contexts for employer and job information are available with live accounts of job experiences in some institutions. This enables students to search through different roles and companies, gaining insights and perspectives from those already in the workplace.

Partnership working

Colleges work in partnership with numerous organisations to meet the skills and wider needs of learners. Examples of some of the joint projects that colleges have successfully been involved in include:

- Joint working with the Metropolitan Police and a local council to inform young people about the dangers of gang violence. Following the gang-related death of a student, a campaign was set up with local partners to support individuals who were worried about gang violence. Students are able to attend sessions at the college run by the police and council.[215]
- Working with local businesses and the council to provide unemployed people with industry specific skills to gain employment. Trainees attend a two week course which is specific to a chosen industry; once this is completed they are guaranteed an interview with an employer on the scheme. The course had a 50 per cent success rate in getting individuals into jobs after the course.[216]
- Recognising the local need for Higher Education in the area, a college worked with the local council, other FE providers and a University to develop a local centre to deliver university courses to the local community and to retain them in the local area once they had graduated.[217]
- Through joint work with local schools, a college has worked to encourage parents to become involved in their children's education, and encourage parents to further their own education and

---

213   Howard, U. (2009).
214   Mauger, S. (2009).
215, 216, 217 CFE (2009b).

skills. Individuals from the local community are trained to deliver training and support to parents within the schools.[218]

There are also numerous examples of colleges working in partnership with employers to develop and deliver training. However, these activities and the other ways in which colleges are meeting the needs of employers are considered in the following section.

Meeting the needs of employers

The development and delivery of training for business is a core element of many colleges' strategies. In some colleges, dedicated business units co-ordinate work with employers within the institution, ensuring a joined-up approach to marketing[219] and the development of a centralised database of employer contacts.[220] Conversely, other colleges organise employer engagement at a curriculum or departmental level, believing that subject specialists will have more credibility with industry. In this case, effective Client Relationship Management (CRM) systems are essential to ensure the activity is coordinated within the college and duplication is avoided. Colleges approach employers to promote their services in a range of ways including telephone calls, company visits, networking at local events, employer liaison groups, promotional material, hosting award days,[221] running open days and providing taster sessions.[222]

Colleges deliver a wide variety of training for employers ranging from standard qualifications through to short courses and bespoke training. Provision can be delivered on site at the college or at an employer's premises. Many employers look to colleges to fulfil their skills needs; in the 2009-10 academic year, two-thirds of large employers who trained their staff did so through a college.[223] According to the 2009 National Employer Skills Survey, the vast

---

218 AoC (2008).
219 Ofsted (2004a).
220 Kelly, S. (2007b).
221 Ofsted (2004a).
222 Kelly, S. (2007b).
223 AoC (2010).

majority of employers (85.1%) that accessed training from FECs were very satisfied or quite satisfied with the quality of the teaching they received.

Alongside delivering FE, 'mixed-economy colleges' also deliver a significant amount of HE provision to individuals and employees through qualifications such as HNDs, HNCs and Foundation degrees (FD). FDs are designed with and for employers and provide a vocational route into higher education for learners. [224] With rising tuition fees in the university sector, learners and employers may increasingly look to colleges for their HE provision. Two FECs have recently been granted powers to award their own Foundation degrees; this frees them from university control and enables them to deliver more flexible, responsive provision.[225]

Colleges also work in partnership with other colleges, private training providers and industry associates to deliver a wider range of provision to employers.[226] Private training providers have considerable expertise in employer engagement and their flexible staffing structures mean that courses can be delivered at short notice and at a convenient time and location. Associates can also offer flexibility, along with practical, up-to-date knowledge which results in greater credibility with employers.[227] Providers working in partnership are also able to spread development costs for new ventures, bid together for public funding and share expertise.[228] In addition, some partnerships co-ordinate their marketing strategies and provide information on joint websites[229] to ensure employers can easily find the information they need from a 'one stop shop' for training in a locality.[230]

In addition, there are instances of colleges partnering with employers to deliver training. The partnership can take a number of forms, but one example is the establishment of a learning centre on an employer's premises. This ensures work-based learners, including those without ICT equipment in their own homes, can access training

---

224   King, M., Widdowson, J. and Brown, R. (2008).
225   TES (2011).
226   LSN (2010).
227   Kelly, S. (2007b).
228, 229 Ofsted (2004a).
230   LSN (2010).

and online resources.[231] Some employers have also made these facilities available to the wider community.[232] Other colleges train employees to become trainers and assessors for the rest of the company. This reduces the amount of time that college staff need to spend on an employer's site and ensures all staff, including shift workers, can access training.[233]

There are also a number of examples of successful partnerships between the private sector and Community Colleges in the United States, which have resulted in highly responsive training provision tailored to the needs of specific communities.[234] Research into these initiatives has identified the essential elements of effective partnership working between a college and a business. These include:

- the identification a 'need' which requires collective action, such as rising unemployment rates;
- the establishment of shared missions and goals;
- the creation of value for all partners involved which are clearly stated;
- strong leadership with organisations; and
- shared governance and accountability for joint projects. [235]

The models that have proved to be particularly successful in the US include: the creation of technology centres offering training and high-tech equipment for use by students and local businesses; workforce development partnerships which design training to meet the needs of numerous businesses as well as create career ladders; welfare to work programmes which combine specific training with the opportunity for learners to move into employment; and business-based scholarship programmes whereby students receive funding from local businesses, and in some instances, are provided with part-time jobs whilst studying.

231   Ofsted (2004a).
232   DIUS, AoC, ALP, and NIACE (2008).
233   Ofsted (2004a).
234, 235 Kisker, C. B. and Carducci, R. (2003).

The above examples highlight activities undertaken by individual colleges and businesses within their localities. One example of a national approach, (although implemented at a local level), to encourage partnerships between the state, colleges and employers is *Skills for America's Future*.[236] This initiative, which is detailed in the case study overleaf involves employers developing relationships with colleges to deliver provision whic\h meets both employers' and learners' needs.

---

236 The Aspen Institute (2011).

Skills for America's Future

'Skills for America's Future' is a national initiative from the Aspen Institute which was launched by President Obama in October 2010. It was designed to connect employers with colleges to ensure learners had the skills employers need and to enable students to gain experience and skills which would help them move into employment. It provides a framework that employers, unions, colleges and other partners can engage with to consider effective solutions to skills issues which have a greater impact than single partnerships:

"Putting resources into the training and development of workers is one of the very best investments we can make. Skills for America's Future brings together government, the private sector, community colleges, and labour to make that happen."

The initial goals for 'Skills for America's Future' include:

- Partnering with community colleges to help achieve an additional 5 million community college degrees and certificates by 2020.
- Ensuring that every state has at least one high-impact partnership between industry and community colleges.

The initiative already has the commitment of some of America's largest companies, including:

- Pacific Gas and Electric Company (PG&E): To expand its energy jobs career pathway over the next three years.
- Gap Inc: To establish new community college partnerships in seven cities by using existing successful practices.
- McDonald's: To double its accelerated language acquisition pathways programme over the next 18 months and make its 'virtual classroom' model available to community colleges.
- United Technologies Corporation (UTC): To work with other employers to replicate its employee scholar and apprenticeship programmes.
- Accenture: To work with other employers and community colleges to expand the reach of its pathways programmes, which prepare students with skills for their first job across industries.

The core activities of the initiative include:

- Providing a national voice on the effectiveness of public/private partnerships in improving the skills, industry-recognised credentials, and employment outcomes of American workers and students.
- Developing a national network of partnerships with a commitment to scaling meaningful and measurable solutions.
- Measuring the impact.
- Sharing knowledge and lessons learned at the community, state, and national level.

Key challenges

The evidence demonstrates that colleges are meeting the learning and wider support needs of their students in a variety of ways, including by harnessing technology, reaching out into communities and working in partnership. However, ensuring learning is as accessible as possible to as wide a range of learners as possible is not without it challenges.

Colleges have developed a wide range of provision designed to meet the differing needs of the communities they serve, including disadvantaged groups. However, there is often a tension between widening participation objectives and pressure to achieve minimum levels of performance; there is evidence that in some instances this has deterred colleges from engaging in activities where the likelihood of student completion is low. For example, a recent report highlighted the risks for colleges when taking on individuals who are unemployed but actively looking for work.[237] Although finding employment is a desirable outcome for the learner, if they drop out of their course in order to take up an employment opportunity, the provider's success levels are negatively affected. This issue was also identified by a training provider delivering Apprenticeships to offenders: *"there were risks involved in them* [the training provider] *taking part in such a scheme...success rates may be lower for this group of people and this could affect their success rates and Minimum Level of Performance. It was felt that Ofsted should take into consideration this group of learners when assessing providers."*[238]

Other tensions exist between the drive towards a more 'customer focussed' approach, underpinned by performance indicators and quality assurance mechanisms, and the delivery of learning provision that addresses the needs of learners and the wider economy. Mechanisms such as Framework for Excellence utilise relatively crude instruments, such as student satisfaction surveys, to gauge student opinion and the extent to which providers are taking account of the learner voice, but these have shown to be flawed. This can lead to

237 CFE (2011).
238 CFE (2010).

'perverse outcomes' and the adoption of 'defensive' strategies which are primarily concerned with achieving high satisfaction ratings and a good position in the league tables. This can discourage open and honest dialogue between providers and learners about weaknesses in student outputs as well as institutional performance.[239]

The introduction of the new Skills Strategy has placed strict parameters on budgets which have also been reduced in size. Recent research outlines how colleges and training providers believe that funding changes will affect some communities more than others, for example ESOL students.[240] According to the new criteria, fully-funded ESOL will only be available for those individuals who are actively seeking employment and are on JSA[241] or ESA[242] (WRAG[243]). This presents colleges with a major challenge as it is likely to dramatically reduce the number of learners who are eligible for funded ESOL provision; this will, in turn, impact on the amount of provision colleges are able to deliver, irrespective of local need/demand. There are concerns that this policy will have a detrimental impact on social cohesion and integration in communities where a large proportion of the population do not speak English as their first language and are not in receipt of work-related benefits. Women are likely to be most affected by the reforms, as they are more likely to be partners of those on low incomes and/or not registered as unemployed.[244]

Colleges also face a number of challenges when responding to articulated need through community outreach activities. Tutors and support staff operating remotely in CLCs assume greater responsibility for providing wider pastoral care for their learners, which has clear implications for both capacity and staff development. As such, staff need to be allocated time and receive adequate training to deliver effective pastoral support; they may also require guidance on managing the formal demands of the programmes alongside the often infor-

---

239 UCU (2010).
240 CFE (2011).
241 Jobseekers allowance.
242 Employment and Support Allowance.
243 Work-related activity group.
244 CFE (2011).

mal relationships they develop with learners.[245] Other agencies working with the community have an important role to play in supporting community-based tutors.[246] However, research suggests that further work is required to alleviate some of the tensions that currently exist between the different partners.

Providing access to support services, such as childcare, in outreach centres presents a further challenge for colleges, as these services are usually confined to main sites. In addition, engaging hard to reach groups on a one-to-one basis, rather than through intermediary agencies, is effective but highly resource intensive.[247] In an environment where providers are experiencing substantial reductions in their core budgets, colleges will be seeking more cost-effective ways of engaging with these groups of learners remotely.

Evidence also suggests that there is a lack of higher level provision delivered in the community in some areas and, as a result, there are limited progression opportunities for learners who choose to study in this way.[248] This issue is exacerbated by learner reluctance to study outside their local area in a more formal educational setting, which does not have the same atmosphere or level of support as the community setting.[249] Although some providers are implementing measures to address this issue, including creating satellite campuses in community settings, the evidence suggests that this is not sufficient to overcome barriers to learner engagement and increase participation by under-represented groups. Forde argues that the development of new learning centres must be located within a wider framework designed to address wider issues of educational inequality.[250] In the absence of a coherent set of policies and strategies, there is a risk that the new campus becomes 'ghettoized'.

Employer engagement is increasingly important for FECs, as an additional and independent source of revenue. However, only a quarter of businesses (27.7%) which provide training for their employees use an FEC. Of those that source their training from elsewhere, over two thirds (41.9%) report that they do not use an FEC because *"the*

245   Gallacher, J., Mayes, T. and Crossan, B. (2007).
246, 247, 248   Hannon, P., Pahl, K., Bird, V., Taylor, C. and Birch, C. (2003).
249   Gallacher, J., Mayes, T. and Crossan, B. (2007).
250   Forde, C. (2000).

courses they provide are not relevant". Challenging these perceptions, raising employers' awareness of the FE offer, and growing their share of the training market, therefore, represent key challenges for some institutions.

Research suggests that there is an inherent tension between what individuals and employers are seeking from adult education and what they are consequently willing to pay for. A further challenge for colleges is, therefore, balancing the needs of these two groups in a co-financing environment.[251]

Finally, it is clear that ICT has had, and continues to have, an impact on the delivery of skills training. Nevertheless, utilising technology to support blended learning approaches is not without its challenges. Access to learning in this way is constrained by attitudes to the use of technology, individual capabilities, access to ICT and the internet, and individual learner styles and preferences. Moreover, the use of technology can have a transformational effect on the way knowledge is created and the relationship between student and teacher; some institutions are, therefore, revisiting traditional approaches to ensure they remain fit for purpose.

Opportunities

In response to the challenges, a number of potential solutions and opportunities are also identified within the literature.

In the current economic climate, there is a great deal of competition for jobs which increasingly demand a wide range of personal attributes as well as technical skills. In order to ensure learners are fully prepared for the labour market, Schuller and Watson argue that the adult curriculum must, therefore, seek to balance generic employability skills with job-specific skills because *"employability involves personal attributes which go well beyond technical or professional skills".*[252] They propose the introduction of a *"citizen's curriculum"*[253] which is designed to equip adult learners with the individual attrib-

---

251   Howard, U. (2009).
252, 253 Schuller, T. and Watson, D. (2009).

utes as well as the employment-specific skills they need, mirroring the 'liberal arts' component offered in many American Community Colleges. Although concerns over employers' willingness to pay for programmes that address generic, transferable skill needs as well as job-specific skills have been raised, the evidence from America suggests that employers are increasingly recognising the need for, and value of, this approach and, as a result, the liberal arts component is growing in popularity.[254]

Research also calls for better progression routes and improved systems of support for learners who make the transition from community learning to more formal educational settings [255, 256] One mechanism for achieving this is to encourage community learners to access some support services, such as childcare, from main sites earlier in their programme in order to become acclimatised to a more formal setting.

Given that ICT is increasingly deployed in the delivery of teaching, further research into the development of pedagogical approaches within adult learning is encouraged. Howard suggests that *"staff should be engaged in research and development to design and deliver flexible, IT-enhanced models and pedagogies for teaching and learning which help adult learners".*[258] This proposition is supported in *Skills for Sustainable Growth* which states that government will look to the sector for ideas on how to *"encourage flexible and innovative approaches to teaching and learning, which…make full use of the potential of technology".*[259]

Finally, as colleges consider ways in which to further develop their employer engagement offer, evidence suggests that colleges should play to their strengths, exploit their unique selling points and/or work in partnership, rather than try to compete directly with other types of provider. Colleges can draw on a range of resources to enhance

254 King, M., Widdowson, J. and Brown, R. (2008.
255 Hannon, P., Pahl, K., Bird, V., Taylor, C. and Birch, C. (2003).
256 Gallacher, J., Mayes, T. and Crossan, B. (2007).
257 Howard, U. (2009).
258 BIS (2010e).
259 AoC (2009b).

their employer engagement strategies including guidance on effective communication with business as well as practical advice for developing provision responsive to employers' needs.[260, 261]

Summary

The relationship between colleges and their communities extends beyond the strategic engagement outlined in the previous chapters to the development and delivery of the adult curriculum. There is evidence to suggest that colleges are working with as well as in their communities to ensure their offer addresses the learning and wider support needs of students, and extends access for those groups who are often under-represented in post-compulsory education. Community outreach work in addition to the application of ICT are integral to current models; however, while the use of technology is likely to increase, there is a risk that resource-intensive outreach work may diminish as budgets are reduced. Successful partnerships are also integral to meeting the needs of different learning communities, including employers, and are set to increase in the context of current reforms, including minimum contract levels, and the implementation of the Qualifications and Credit framework. Effective links between FECs and other learning providers, including the private sector have been established; partnerships between FECs, community organisations and employers are also widespread.

Although colleges are highly successful at meeting the needs of a wide range of learners, some key challenges remain and new challenges are emerging as a result of the reforms set out in the current skills strategy. These include reconciling the tensions that currently exist between minimum performance levels and indictors and widening participation objectives; responding to the needs of communities within a straightened funding regime which is likely to result in a reduction in resources for outreach and in the number of learners eligible for public support; and the demands of employers with the needs of individual learners. There are also practical challenges asso-

---

260 Ofsted (2004a).
261 Kelly, S. (2007b).

ciated with staff training, learner progression, and effective employer engagement. The evidence suggests that innovation and technology offer part of the solution, however, more radical changes to operating models may be required if the full benefits are to be realised.

6 Impacting on communities

Colleges impact upon the personal as well as the professional development of learners through a wide ranging curriculum. However, the extent to which this impact extends beyond the level of the individual to their communities and the economy as a whole remains a matter for debate

This section considers the ways in which colleges have an impact on learners, the employers they work with and the extent to which this impact extends to the wider communities they serve and bring local economic benefits. It also highlights national and international examples of current practice and examines how college resources could be further utilised to support wider community objectives not directly linked to learning and skills.

Impact on the learner

The impact that skills and qualifications have on individual learners, including their employment prospects[262] and earning potential[263] is well documented. However, there is also evidence to suggest that learning at college, whether through academic, vocational or informal provision, has wider benefits for learners which extend beyond skills to the social as well as economic well-being of individuals.[264] As a result, research suggests that:

> "the learning and skills sector is well placed to play an active part in citizen engagement activities in the coming years...The sector has a track record of being responsive to change; this suggests the sector can adapt to the policy developments of the Coalition's Big Society."[265]

---

262 Carpentieri, J. D. and Vorhaus, J. (2010).
263 Feinstein, L., Budge, D., Vorhaus, J. and Duckworth, K. (2008).
264 Carpentieri, J. D. and Vorhaus, J (2010).
265 LSIS (2010a).

Social deprivation is perceived to be at the heart of much of the breakdown of civil society and the FE sector has an important role to play in reducing this problem. The provision of basic skills training and professional vocational development assists individuals to improve their lives and achieve sustainable employment.[267] It is also asserted that *"those individuals who are better educated have higher levels of civic participation and community leadership"*.[268]

Adult learning can be positively associated with increased life satisfaction, social mobility and improved health. One study that compared those who studied adult literacy and numeracy with the outcomes of those who did not found that the learners had increased self-esteem, improved commitment to education and training, increased literacy and numeracy skills, improved health and increased independence.[269]

Further research has found a link between adult participation in FE and increased civic and/or political engagement as well as changes in social attitudes.[270] Although cause and effect is difficult to determine, it is argued that participation in FE can enhance an individual's social capital through the development of social competencies, extending social networks and promoting social norms.[271] This can lead to increased racial tolerance and the prevention of extremist attitudes; however, a link between participation in FE and changes in extremist views that have already been formed has not been established.

It has also been argued that engagement in learning can have a positive impact on crime levels. Individuals actively engaged in learning have less opportunity to commit crime; the likelihood that they will commit crime in the future is also reduced because the additional skills and/or qualifications they achieve enhance their opportunities to gain employment. It has been suggested that individual engagement

266 157 Group (2010b).
267 Commission on Integration and Cohesion. (2007).
268 157 Group (2010b).
269 Carpentieri, J. D. and Vorhaus, J. (2010).
270 The majority of research relates to all forms of FE.
271 Carpentieri, J. D. and Vorhaus, J. (2010).

in learning can also have a positive impact on the choices and behaviours of other family members as a high proportion of offending is strongly concentrated in families.[272]

In addition to reducing offending behaviours within families, the benefits of adult learning can also have wider impacts, such as positively affecting the educational attainment of future generations. Children of parents with higher level qualifications tend to go on to study at higher levels. This is attributed to a range of factors, including: individuals with higher qualifications tend to earn more and are able to provide their children with materials and resources to aid their education; parental attitudes towards learning are more positive and/or parents are more likely to read to their children.[273, 274]

Although learners experience a wide range of benefits of learning, the extent and strength of the impact is dependent on how long the learner was in some form of education and also whether that learning experience was a positive one.[275] Research has found that early years and compulsory education have the biggest impacts; yet even a short course in adult learning can have beneficial effects, with impacts being greatest for those who were previously educationally disadvantaged.

Impact on the community

The notion of the 'Big Society' is underpinned by a belief that increased participation in learning can benefit wider communities by encouraging social stability and greater community cohesion. Colleges are at the heart of their communities and play a vital role in ensuring that the wider community is prepared to take advantage of the empowerment explicit in the new Big Society policy. Current research for the Department for Business, Innovation and Skills (BIS) suggests that colleges are already working to improve levels of responsiveness and engage communities in shaping local provision.[276]

272 Feinstein, L. (2002).
273 Feinstein, L., Budge, D., Vorhaus, J. and Duckworth, K. (2008.
274 Feinstein, L., Duckworth, K. and Sabates, R. (2004).
275 Feinstein, L., Budge, D., Vorhaus, J. and Duckworth, K. (2008).
276 CFE (2011).

In the discussion of a future curriculum for the FE sector, Howard proposes a 'citizens' curriculum' which has at its core the aim *"to create a more inclusive society, [by] strengthening people's sense of agency and belonging in a democratic society, [and] developing the contribution that adults make as citizens".*[277] Ofsted, reporting on social responsibility and community cohesion, noted that *"effective* [educational] *settings provided a broad and flexible curriculum... [which] prepared learners well to participate actively in society".*[278] This could include supporting students to make a direct contribution, for example, through volunteering, which brings positive outcomes for learners, the college as an institution, and the wider community.[279] One example of where citizenship is seen to be key to colleges is through the Learning by Volunteering project in Scotland as shown in the case study overleaf.[280]

However, the value that colleges bring to a specific community is difficult to measure because of the diversity of adult learners, different course and institutional objectives along with other influences. As a result, little research has been conducted into the impact that colleges have in this regard and opinion remains divided as to whether investment in the development of an individual can be expected to have a broader impact at community level.

Schuller argues: *"because it is individuals who learn, the whole argument around the contribution that lifelong learning can make... is often seen as a matter of individual agency...but we should not believe that learning has its effects purely by changing individual attitudes and behaviour."*[281] Others believe that the development of social capital through individual learning activities does not necessarily equate to increased social capital at community level: *"there is no significant relationship between mean levels of education in a society and levels of trust or tolerance."*[282] The gap in the evidence base has been acknowledged within the FE sector, with college principals

---

277 Howard, U. (2009).
278 Ofsted (2010).
279 Volunteering England and LSC (2008).
280 Learning by Volunteering (2011).
281 Schuller, T. (2009).
282 Green, A., Preston, J. and Sabates, R. (2003).

Learning by Volunteering, Scotland

The Learning by Volunteering project started in late 2009 and was launched in March 2010. It was a partnership project between Angus College (lead partner), Adam Smith College, Langside College and Scotland's Colleges and funded by the Scottish Funding Council.

The aim of the project is to *"enhance and add value to the existing work of colleges by creating a culture of volunteering which articulates with citizenship, employability, essential skills development and utilisation and implementation of the curriculum for excellence framework. Actively driving forward the opportunity for learners to volunteer; adding value to their formal learning experience and recognising this, will enhance the whole college experience for learners."*

The role of the three colleges was to drive forward learner volunteering in their college to enhance their formal learning. The project is built on the premise that formal learning can be enhanced by engaging in volunteering activities, alongside developing the active citizenship, employability and essential skills development, core skills development and lifelong learning. A wide range of materials have been develop to ensure the learning from this project can be shared and the resources and toolkit are available here: **http://learningbyvolunteering.org/**

As part of the project, an award ceremony was held to recognise the volunteering that students were undertaking. Angus College's Volunteering Projects Officer Stewart Roy commented:

"This year's Student Volunteer Award Ceremony has been a real success. We had over 90 students being formally recognised for their volunteering efforts across Angus and with the success of our first Volunteer Recruitment Fair which followed the ceremony we now expect these numbers to increase. Volunteering has allowed our students to put theory from their learning into practice, whilst at the same time giving something back to the community of Angus. Volunteering is very much on Angus College's agenda and we are working hard with our other partners nationally to support Scotland's Colleges to get on board with developing student volunteering."

agreeing that *"the sector… punches below its weight because it does less around measuring* [the] *social impact"*[283] of its activities.

Although more needs to be done, there is evidence to suggest that some institutions are beginning to develop mechanisms to measure the impact they are having on their local communities. These include perception surveys and websites akin to 'trip advisor' which enable learners and community members to provide feedback on their experiences of the provider, which can be accessed by the general public.

A number of colleges nationally and internationally are also trying to evidence the social as well as the economic impact they are having on their local area. They have attempted to calculate the Social Return on Investment of the college to show if there is a return on the amount of public money being spent. The studies have outlined the impact they are having on the economy through creating full- and part-time jobs and through the contribution that the learners can have on the economy once they are trained. The studies also highlight the wider impact that colleges can have on an area such as those outlined previously - improving health and reducing unemployment and crime - all of which can help to reduce public expenditure in these areas.[284]

Utilising resources

Alongside provision to support skills development and citizen engagement, colleges are considering the contribution that their capital assets could make to community development. In his report, *Realising the potential: a review of the future role of further education colleges*, Foster notes the difficulties encountered in attempting to gather comprehensive information on the use of college assets.[285] However, Howard suggests that the plant and estate of colleges are currently underused and proposes that colleges should work with other organisations in order to better utilise these resources.[286] Many commentators have noted that colleges are ideally placed to provide *"spaces*

---

283 HayGroup (2010).
284 AoC (2009a).
285 Foster, A. (2005).
286 Howard, U. (2009).

to draw communities together".[287] However, broadening the use of college assets is not without costs, including those relating to utilities, security, insurance and personnel. These have to be reconciled with potential cost savings in other areas of the public sector and the wider benefits that could be achieved at the local level.

Colleges not only have physical resources which can be utilised by communities and local groups, they also have expertise, knowledge and capacity which can be used to support wider social and economic objectives. An example of how resources are being utilised in this way is provided in the case study of Niagara College, Ontario, Canada overleaf

There are also examples of how colleges in the USA make their resources available to communities, including, the college library, meeting room space and the book store.[288] In addition to providing research services to businesses, other organisations in the UK are also utilising their resources to support SMEs. One scheme is illustrated on page 164 in the case study drawn from the higher education sector.

---

287 LSIS (2010a).
288 deCastro, B. S. and Karp, M. M. (2008).

Niagara College, Canada

Niagara Research is part of Niagara College's Research & Innovation Division in Ontario, Canada. In partnership with businesses and/or community partners they undertake applied research in areas of relevance and importance to the economic health of the Niagara region. The college utilise their existing expert staff and students to conduct research projects; recent figures indicate that each semester between 20 and 40 students are employed and a further 600 students are involved in course-based projects with over 50 industry partners.

The main aims of Niagara Research are to:

- support community and economic development in Niagara, Ontario, and Canada;
- enhance the quality of academic programmes and the professional development of college personnel; and
- support the development of applied research skills of students.

They seek to achieve these aims by:

- supporting economic development in the Niagara Region and beyond through industry partnerships for appropriately applied research initiatives;
- conducting applied research and knowledge/technology transfer activities that help business, industry and the community develop and improve products, processes, and services, solve problems and meet goals;
- encouraging opportunities for Niagara College staff and students to work with business, industry and the community to conduct research; and
- developing provincial, and where appropriate, national and international networks and alliances, with institutions with similar goals to advance research in the college setting.

The research activities are driven by the needs of the industries the college works with. The college acts as a hub for receiving research grants, conducting outreach activities to determine business /industry research and development needs or priorities, and managing intellectual property issues. It enables their students to gain practical work experience whilst supporting industry to develop new products, evaluate services or develop strategies.

More information about the work Niagara College is doing can be found here:

www.niagaracollege.ca/research/about/strategicdirection.html

De Montfort University Business Services, Leicester, UK

De Montfort University offers a range of courses and training to employers alongside undertaking research in a wide range of business sectors. In addition, the University's Innovation Centre offers a range of services including: full tenancy agreements for business start-ups; meeting and training room space for hire; and a Virtual Tenancy package for those who want a more flexible workspace for their business

The fully furnished workspaces enable new or emerging design, IT and technology based businesses to rent an office for approximately three years. The package includes:

- Broadband access
- Reception service
- On-site business advice and support
- Links to the university's facilities and expertise
- PR support
- Legal advice surgery – provided by Smith Partnership
- Finance support
- Marketing support

The Virtual Tenancy offer is available to those who are starting a business but cannot commit to a full tenancy agreement. For a monthly fee businesses can benefit from:

- Telephone answering service
- A postal address with post forwarded weekly
- A discount on meeting room hire
- Free use of the reception cafe areas and Innovation Centre lounge
- Free access to business workshops and seminars

Alongside the benefits to community groups and businesses, sharing resources and the associated cost savings can be implemented between colleges and/or other educational institutions.[289] Recent research in the US found that community colleges were forming partnerships with other colleges and institutions for this purpose. For example, a group of community colleges and a university worked in partnership to purchase an e-learning system which saved the partners nearly $500,000 annually. Another example showed how a college and the area's centre for economic development pooled resources to

---

289 deCastro, B. S. and Karp, M. M. (2008).

create a building to deliver programmes, alongside housing a number of partners including: chamber of commerce, the economic development department and an education centre.

The case study overleaf shows how colleges can also work in partnership to meet a wider range of needs for their local communities.[290] The partners make key contribution to local and regional priorities for improving education and share expertise around leadership and volunteering.

Impact on businesses

Some colleges capture evidence of employer satisfaction with training in a range of ways including formal questionnaires or employer liaison meetings; whereas other providers do not formally measure this and take repeat business as an indicator of employer satisfaction.[291] However, satisfaction ratings only provide an indication of the extent to which employers are satisfied with delivery; they are not a measure of impact.

Until recently, colleges and other providers demonstrating effective practice in employer engagement and responsiveness had the opportunity to be recognised for their efforts in the form of the Training Quality Standard (TQS).[292] TQS was developed to recognise and celebrate the best organisations delivering *"high quality, high impact training"*.[293] In order to achieve recognition, aspects of a provider's *"responsiveness, flexibility, expertise and commitment to continuous improvement"* were examined.[294] During this process providers were required to demonstrate that the training they delivered was impacting on the individual learner as well as the business by meeting identified

---

290   This case study is a summary of a case study published in 157 Group (2010a).

291   Ofsted (2004a).

292   The Skills funding Agency withdrew funding for the Training Quality Standard in April 2011. Although certification is no longer available, alternative support and recognition is being offered though a new Improvement Framework, Training Excellence (www.trainingexcellence.co.uk).

293, 294   Training Quality Standard (2011).

Leading the way in transforming standards in city schools, Birmingham

Birmingham Metropolitan College has become part of a partnership (including a university and another college) to transform education in the local area lead by Birmingham City Council. Its role is to 'ensure all schools are 'centres of learning fit for the 21st century'.

The partnership is supporting National Challenge Schools and tackling the high proportion of pupils who do not gain five or more GCSEs (including English and Maths) in some institutions. BMC is providing strategic leadership to two schools where the proportion of pupils not achieving five or more GCSEs is more than 70% after three years of extra funding. The college regards this work as part of their mission to meet the needs of the learners and the local economy.

"The college plays a key role in contributing to local and regional priorities, raising achievement, and increasing participation at post-16. It also has strategic partnerships with a number of local and regional universities such as Aston and Birmingham City Universities."

The college also have plans to sponsor an Academy in the area and support the city's ambition to develop STEM subjects: "We offer fantastic opportunities in terms of digital technology. We opened our Samsung Digital Service Academy in April and have a national contract to train Sky apprentices."

needs. This recognises that skills development and/or qualifications do not automatically have an impact on a business or its productivity.

It should be noted that measuring the impact of training, in terms of return on investment, remains a key challenge for learning providers and employers, not least because any number of factors are likely to contribute to improved performance. As colleges become increasing accountable to local communities, including employers, and the market for skills becomes even more competitive, colleges may need to turn their attention to the development of more effective ways of demonstrating impact. Good practice suggests that this involves working more closely with employers at the outset to identify and agree what success looks; these measures should then inform both the design and delivery of the programme and the associated learning outcomes.[295]

---

295 Currie, A. and Brown, D. (2009).

Impact on the local economy

Whilst little has been written on the impact of FECs on their local economy, a number of recent reports undertaken by EMSI have attempted to measure the economic impact of FECs within *specific regions* in England. They suggest that FECs impact on the local economy in a number of ways, including directly as an employer and a purchaser of services, and indirectly as a supplier of skilled labour and services to the community.

FECs are often one of the major employers in their geographical area and, as such, make a substantial contribution to their local economy by providing employment for a wide range of individuals. Colleges employ 245,000 people nationally, 128,000 of whom are teachers and lecturers.[296] Research suggests that colleges can boost local income through staff salaries and college operations by up to £24.2 million.[297]

Local spending by learners on transport, food outlets, retailers and leisure activities[298] also makes a significant contribution to the local economy and is estimated to boost income by up to £1.8 million in some areas.[299] Once students graduate into the local labour market they continue to contribute to the local economy. Data from 2006/7 showed that college learners contributed approximately two per cent of the national GDP, which yielded an average eight per cent return on investment to the government. In addition, research suggests that higher qualified individuals experience better health, lower rates of unemployment, higher earning potential, and make fewer demands on other social services.[300] By equipping learners with the skills and attributes they need to live healthy and productive lives, FECs help to generate revenue as well as make significant savings for the public purse.

Finally many colleges also provide services to the public, such as restaurants and hair and beauty salons, at reduced prices[301]

---

296 AoC (2011).
297 EMSI (2008).
298 AoC (2009a).
299 EMSI (2008).
300 Widdowson, J. (2010).
301 Collinson, M. and Collinson, D. (2005).

and support local businesses through the provision of work placements.

Summary

There is evidence to suggest that adult learning can have a range of benefits for the learner, both personally and professionally, which can also extend to those in their family. Although opinion is divided on the extent to which individual benefits impact the wider community, colleges, through their work with learners and partner organisations, contribute to improved community cohesion and social integration. Further research is required to produce more robust data on the social as well as the economic returns of adult learning.

Colleges also have a direct impact on local businesses, both as purchasers of products and services and suppliers of training and skilled labour. However, the extent to which training impacts on productivity is mediated by the effectiveness of the mechanisms in place for the deployment and utilisation of skills.

There are many examples of how colleges and universities in the UK and internationally utilise their resources for the benefit of their wider communities, including businesses. This includes the provision of physical space, business support services, and research and knowledge transfer. These links offer a 'win win' situation for all parties, both financially and in relation to the continuous professional development of staff and students.

Colleges are, therefore, more than just providers of learning and skills. They add value to the communities they serve by contributing to wider social and economic agendas.

7 Governance and accountability

As a consequence of the drive to increase accountability to local communities, approaches to college governance and leadership need revisiting. This section explores the models currently in use and the implications for accountability structures in a changed environment.

Governance

The roots of the term 'governance' can be traced back to Latin and ancient Greek words meaning to 'steer' or 'guide'. In the past, the concept of 'governance' has been closely associated with the act of 'government' and primarily concerned with constitutional and legal issues. However, more recently a clearer distinction has been drawn between the modes and manner of governing (governance) and the institutions and agents charged with governing (government). This differentiation recognises that while governments have a governing role, the process of governance involves a wider range of individuals, groups and organisations and takes place at a number of levels, including at the level of an individual institution such as an FEC. [302]

A review of the literature identified numerous models of governance currently in operation. Structures are primarily determined by the size of the college; however, in general, around 20 governors serve as non-executive members of a Board. With the exception of the principal, senior managers within the college are not allowed to sit on the Board. Therefore, the majority of governors, including the Chair, are external and independent of the college. Generally, these individuals are business and community leaders with expertise in managing large or complex organisations and a commitment to serving a public service. Boards of governors typically convene once a quarter, although

302 Jessop, B. (1998).

organisational performance is reviewed more frequently.[303] Strategic plans tend to be revised every 3-5 years. However, recent research has found that in a dynamic policy and regulatory context many FECs are revising their strategies annually in order to effectively respond to these changes and the wider economy.[304]

Boards of Governors, however they are constituted, have a crucial role to play within colleges and a lack of effective governance and strategic leadership is a key contributing factor within failing institutions.[305] Strong governance provides strategic direction by shaping as well as actively supporting the achievement of a shared vision for the college and has a key role in monitoring the academic and financial performance of an institution. Although the extent to which governors have direct links with curriculum areas varies, the most effective governors have a good grasp of the curriculum and the extent and nature of students' achievements. Finally, good governance makes a significant contribution to quality assurance; governors, who are aware of the relative strengths and limitations of an institution, act as 'critical friends' and, amongst other things, constructively review and evaluate self-assessment reports.

Research suggests that three models of governance predominate in England:

- the 'hands-on' approach, whereby the board or governing body become involved in management as well as governance;
- the 'Agency Theory' approach, whereby there is strict separation between the Board and management and the principal acts as an agent of the Board; and
- the 'stewardship' approach, whereby the interests of all those involved in the organisation are shared and represented by a wide range of members on a large Board.[306]

---

303 Schofield A., Matthews, J. and Shaw, S. (2009).
304 CFE (2011).
305 Ofsted (2004b).

At present, the stewardship approach is most wide-spread. Given the current drive for colleges to become increasingly engaged with and more accountable to their local communities, this model offers colleges a number of advantages. A key strength of this approach is that it is based on the principles of co-operation, collaboration and mutual goals, which foster positive team spirit. All parties strive to achieve the same objectives, so there is little need for close control; instead focus is directed towards attaining desired outcomes. The collaborative nature of this model also helps to accelerate decision making and the close involvement of senior managers ensures strong links between the college decision making body and the Board are maintained. However, there are also a number of limitations to this approach. Boards tend to be comprised of a large number of governors and can often become unwieldy; this can reduce operational effectiveness. A lack of distinction between governance and management can also lead to duplication and uncertainty in relation to responsibilities and/or accountability. Moreover, entirely shared objectives can undermine the strength of strategic support provided by a governing body of this nature, as ideas and strategic direction are not challenged and subject to the same level of pressure testing as in other models.[307]

As the freedoms and flexibilities for colleges extend and the opportunities for partnership and collaboration widen to encompass organisations - including those in the private sector which operate in different ways and have different priorities - it is imperative that colleges seek to further develop and maintain appropriate governance structures. NFER suggests that the focus should be on developing processes (agreeing outcomes, allocating resources) and frameworks (elucidating protocols, roles and responsibilities and accountability for progress).[308] However, it is also suggested that a college's Board of Governors *"can help further social integration by reflecting in their membership the major groups represented in their communities"* and that within current models of governance *"giving real power to college governors is one way of reconnecting people with the policy process."*[309] This is particularly pertinent

---

306, 307   Schofield A., Matthews, J. and Shaw, S. (2009).
308   Lord, P., Martin, K., Atkinson, M. and Mitchell, H. (2009).
309   157 Group (2010b).

in the context of the Coalition Government's 'Big Society' agenda.

Although there is general agreement that increased diversity of college boards is desirable, it also presents real challenges at a time when traditional understandings of college leadership and the role of governors are being challenged. For example, it is proposed that college governors assume a *"critical role in developing a meaningful relationship with the LEP."*[310] The role of governor in some contexts is, therefore, evolving from 'guardian of the college' to 'partner in wider communities'.[311] As a result, the initial recruitment of, and ongoing support for, governors must be given careful consideration.

At present, it is not unusual for boards to be dominated by white, middle-class retired men, reflecting the skewed nature of the working population at senior levels.[312] Ofsted argues that further work is therefore required to ensure college governor recruitment strategies are capable of targeting and attracting suitably qualified applicants able to give their time freely and reflect the diversity of local communities.[313] Evidence of more innovative approaches to recruitment is beginning to emerge, including the appointment of student and staff board members; however, initial recruitment and retention remains a key challenge. In addition, research suggests that staff and students can feel inhibited when speaking in front of their superiors and this can limit the extent and effectiveness of their participation. Once recruited, LSIS and AoC advocate the implementation of a formal performance review process for governors to ensure they perform effectively in what is likely to be an increasingly demanding role.[314]

Given the large number and range of communities some colleges serve, it is unlikely that all colleges could adequately ensure their Board was fully representative while remaining effective, even if recruitment strategies were improved. In addition, the task of reconciling the myriad of potentially conflicting operating values with the principles underpinning the mission and vision of the college should not be underestimated.[315] Colleges may, therefore, wish to consider

---

310   BIS (2010e).
311   Gleeson, D., Abbott, I. and Hill, R. (2009).
312   Schofield A., Matthews, J. and Shaw, S. (2009).
313   Ofsted (2010).
314, 315 Schofield A., Matthews, J. and Shaw, S. (2009).

alternative models of governance which would improve accountability to local communities without the need to form large and unwieldy Boards. Howard proposes accountability structures which are *"more lateral and less vertical"*, such as multi-stakeholder, mutuals or membership organisations.[316] These models would enable organisations (such as employers and employee representative bodies) which prioritise learning to contribute to strategic planning and decision making. It would also help emphasise that accountability to learners and the community is of upmost importance.

A further approach has been inspired by the work of John Carver.[317] This model is premised on a belief that the local community 'owns' the college, and accordingly, that the college should be accountable to that community. However, this model requires considerable support from the principal and is 'explicitly hierarchical', dissuading some colleges from adopting it.[318] Models which entail partnership across wider community-facing groups have also been considered. It has been argued that local authorities should have more responsibility in linking educational services to other services, and thus encourage health and cultural groups to be involved. In this way, collaboration could help make *"lifelong opportunities available that can meet identified needs and support community well-being."*[319]

The implementation of alternative approaches would require a review of the structures which provide the legislative framework for colleges; however, with the Coalition signalling explicit support for innovative models of public service delivery, such as *"co-ops, mutuals, charities and social enterprises,"*[320] the sector could reasonably anticipate a positive response to innovations in relation to governance and accountability.

316 Howard, U. (2009).
317 Policy Governance (2011).
318 Schofield A., Matthews, J. and Shaw, S. (2009).
319 Schuller, T. and Watson, D. (2009).
320 Cabinet Office (2010)

Leadership

Effective governance acts as an adjunct to successful leadership. Sawbridge[321] identified that three main types of leadership are found in FECs in the UK: transactional, instructional and transformational, which are outlined below:[322, 323]

- The transactional approach is the dominant model and characterised as managerial, functional or action-based leadership. The model focuses on team working and the leader's role is to: balance the needs of the whole team, the task on which the team is engaged, and the individual needs of team members. The transactional model attaches significant importance to the development of leadership skills among leaders. Whilst there is an emphasis on the development of personal attributes, such as the ability to motivate and influence others, which have the potential to reflect leadership behaviours, they are of secondary importance to leadership skills. As a result, leaders perform management activities in a rather prescribed manor.
- The instructional leadership model resembles a top-down hierarchical approach to leadership. Unlike the transactional model, the instructional model focuses on the development of leadership behaviours to influence, support and monitor staff, particularly in the planning and delivery of teaching and learning and, as such, relates to the leader's role in promoting learner outcomes. This model is less prominent in UK colleges.
- Lastly, transformational leadership centres on leadership behaviours and the ability of leaders to empower, motivate and support others to promote change, ensure higher performance by both students and staff, and achieve organisational goals. Whilst this model is widely advocated in education, it is not clear how widely it is practiced. The model is also criticised for its focus on continuous improvement and ignoring the importance of teaching and learning.

---

321 Sawbridge, S. J. (2000).
322 Sawbridge, S. J. (2001).
323 Peeke, G. (2003).

Although the transactional model is prominent in UK colleges, Sawbridge argues that the characteristics associated with effective leadership are more closely aligned with the instructional and transformational models.[324]

Historic notions of leadership are losing traction; leadership is now rarely something that is vested in a single charismatic and transformational individual but is increasingly distributed across the organisation to managers at different levels.[325]

"FE leadership may be much more about collaboration, cooperation and facilitation, about brokering and coordination, enhancing interdependence and developing reciprocity within and between communities."[326]

The redistribution of the leadership function is necessitated by a substantial growth in the range of responsibilities college principals assume, including the requirement to develop and maintain partnerships. As a result, college leaders are seeking to balance their involvement with their communities, both internal and external to the organisation, and ensure individuals are suitably empowered to address the tasks and challenges they face in their particular localities.[327] The most successful leaders achieve this by adopting an open and consultative style, engaging staff in strategic planning and decision-making, ensuring clarity of individual roles, responsibilities and accountabilities, and prioritising learner achievement.[328]

Whilst recognising that different demands are placed on individuals at strategic and operational levels of management, it is suggested that distributing leadership within colleges brings benefits both in providing strategic leaders with the time and opportunity to engage with external communities, and in extending responsibility throughout the organisation. These benefits are particularly noticeable in smaller FECs, where increasing demands for external engagement may be detrimental to the ability of the senior management team to respond

---

324   Sawbridge, S. J. (2001).
325, 326, 327 Collinson, M. and Collinson, D. (2005).
328   Ofsted (2004c).

to the internal community of staff and students. It is also argued that there are clear links between leadership and the quality of teaching and learning in a college. Effective leadership has been shown to positively affect the recruitment and selection of teaching staff and their subsequent growth and development as well as helping to create an environment in which teachers are motivated to give their best.[329]

However, developing distributed models of leadership also presents a key challenge to the sector. Significant investment in staff development for leaders at all levels, and principals in particular, is required to ensure they have the appropriate combination of technical and relational skills to do the job effectively.[330] FE leaders themselves suggest extending coaching, mentoring and learning networks to make best use of the experience of the sector's most effective leaders.[331]

Collinson and Collinson suggest that utilising a model that employs both 'distributed leadership' (the vertical dispersal of authority and responsibility) and 'shared leadership' (the horizontal dispersal of the same) develops both a culture of collective responsibility within the organisation and the individual leadership capacities of those involved.[332] This is supported by the canon of literature on the psychology of leadership, which concludes that *"it is probable that anyone can act as an effective leader in the right group at the right time"*.[333] The National College for School Leadership give further weight to this contention, suggesting that *"seeing leadership as fluid, rather than located in specific formal roles or positions"* is of critical importance.[334] In practical terms, distributing and sharing leadership within the internal community of the college may be undertaken through actions such as extending leading and management programmes beyond the organisation's middle management.

---

329 157 Group and CfBT (2011).
330 LSIS (2010d).
331 Gibney, J., Yapp, C., Trickett, L. and Collinge, C. (2009).
332 Collinson, D. (ed.) (2008).
333 See Brown (1985) and Turner (1991), cited in: Gross, R. (1996).
334 Bennett, N., Wise, C., Woods, P. and Harvey, J. (2003).

Accountability

As noted previously, current policy is moving away from the concept of a centrally-planned skills system. As a result, greater responsibility for planning and shaping skills provision is being devolved to communities in order to address locally-articulated need. Coupled with the implementation of a credit-based system of vocational qualifications and a growing emphasis on the development of more learner-centred models, these drivers are likely to shift the accountability away from government and funding agencies with a greater emphasis on accountability to learners and colleges' wider communities.[335]

> "The adult education movement was not born of government, but of the people. And its primary accountability today should be not to the government, but to the people it serves."[336]

However, the shift in accountability could create tensions for providers where success in the eyes of their communities, conflicts with performance measures imposed by funding bodies and/or national skills priorities. For example, we highlighted earlier in this report that in some areas with large migrant populations, demand for ESOL is likely to be substantial but not all potential learners will be eligible for funding under the new arrangements. In addition, the term 'accountability' in this context, is one which is open to interpretation. Despite available government information on its intended meaning, the views of colleges differ greatly. A recent report found that some colleges are wary that it will involve increased local authority control; whilst others perceive it could lead to greater performance management requirements.[337]

In their role as strategic leaders, 'accountability' is, and will continue to be, a key consideration for governors in particular. We noted earlier that student satisfaction surveys are commonly used to monitor and assess institutional performance and impact; in the future their use is likely to be extended in order to demonstrate

---

335, 336   BIS (2010e).
337   CFE (2011).

accountability.[338] However, the customer base is wider than just students, necessitating additional approaches. One concept currently being explored is the 'Community Scorecard', designed to both strengthen and demonstrate providers' contribution and local account-ability to their communities.[339] While this is still in development, it is likely that the scorecard will take into account a variety of measures, which could include: customer satisfaction; stakeholder views; commu-nity needs; level of volunteering activity; number and range of events open to the community; the extent to which patterns of participation could be mapped to areas of disadvantage; and the extent to which the provider's curriculum is seen to be meeting the needs of the community.

Given that colleges vary greatly in terms of the communities they service and the services they provide, a framework which can be tailored to the individual circumstances of the college is more likely to be effective than one that is designed to be 'one size fits all'. In addition, whatever system is finally implemented, it will be important to ensure that the administrative burden on providers is minimised and that the process is simple, straightforward and understood by everyone, includ-ing the communities that will make use of the information. On the basis of the information produced, it is realistic to assume that communities may seek to actively influence college policy and practice and this could result in challenges to the leadership of college principals and gover-nors.[340] A further consideration is the extent to which colleges are equipped to listen and respond to challenges of this nature, and as with the public sector generally, this process will require skilled manage-ment. Colleges may need to assess the skills their staff will need to ensure they are equipped to deal with the challenges.[341]

Although accountability is a key responsibility for governors and college principals, staff at all levels have a role in ensuring that the organisation achieves the strategic and operational objectives against which it will be held to account. The development of effective accountability structures *within* institutions is, therefore, equally as important as, and intrinsically linked to, the development of *outward*

338 IOE (2010).
339 LSIS and UKCES (2011).
340 BIS (2010e).
341 LSIS (2010a).

facing models. It is important that colleges set clear parameters for staff roles and responsibilities and create an environment in which staff are empowered to act autonomously in the pursuit of their agreed targets and goals.[342] However, it is important to note this approach encourages risk-taking. Although this can lead to innovation, failure is always an option and this should be acknowledged and taken into account in any assessment of performance. Good communication and a high degree of trust are, therefore, integral to the success of this model.[343] In addition, the concept of 'individual professionalism' is likely to require a shift in attitudes and organisational culture in contexts where staff are more accustomed to tightly managed and prescribed ways of working and vertical, rather than lateral models of accountability.[344]

An example of a college which has a self regulatory process to ensuring its curriculum is accountable to its community is presented in the case study overleaf. The freedom from top-down control extended to the college, its journey to self-regulation and its ownership and responsibility for its own performance show what is possible and provides valuable learning opportunities for English colleges seeking to increase their accountability to their communities. The case study also provides an example of how it possible for colleges to develop their own self improvement processes without the intervention of government. This supports the notion that self governance and regulation only works if organisations are provided with the capacity to act independently. However, it is worth noting that the government does regulate some aspects of the college's activity, which presents a co-regulation scenario. The lessons learned here are also valuable for English colleges. However, in England where there are many providers operating in a culture of comprehensive government imposed regulations, it is suggested that the co-regulation model is more likely to be one of co-authored agreement, whereby the government and colleges develop regulations in collaboration.[345, 346]

---

342 Ofsted (2004c).
343 Schuller, T. and Watson, D. (2009).
344 IOE (2010).
345 Hubert, P., Sallis, E. and Jones, G. (2009).
346 Howard, U. (2009).

Self regulation of curriculum offering: Highlands College, Jersey, Channel Islands

Highlands College is the only Further Education College situated on the island of Jersey. It provides an English curriculum and in many respects is akin to a typical English FE college; however, its accountability structure is different. Given that Jersey is self-governing, Highlands College is part of the State of Jersey Education, Sport and Culture Department. Whilst it is subject to the State of Jersey's financial, procurement and human resource regulation, the Department has imposed limited curriculum regulation; instead the college is trusted to understand communities' needs and develop a corresponding curriculum.

Despite having a level of autonomy and a monopoly on the Island, Highlands College is focused on serving the needs of its 90,000 strong community and delivers a wide and diverse range of provision to 6,000 students each year. The College is empowered by the State to liaise directly with businesses and learners to determine its offer and endeavours to respond to identified learning needs in positive and innovative ways, while maintaining quality. For example the College is currently partnered with more than 350 providers.

In addition to shaping its curriculum offer to meet the needs of its community, Highlands College is committed to self improvement and has developed an approach which has placed it in a position of self regulation. Highlands College's journey to self-improvement began in 1997 when the College decided to undergo a voluntary inspection against the Common Inspection Framework to benchmark itself against English FECs. Over the years the College's approach to self-improvement developed. In 2004 they arrived at an approach that still used the Common Inspection Framework as a basis, but they also embraced Supported Self Improvement. As part of this process they underwent annual reviews which focused on two out of six curriculum areas. In addition to self assessment, each review took a two part structure: the first involved a visit from a critical friend who provided several hypotheses which were then tested at the second visit, some months later.

The period between the two visits provided the College with time to implement rapid development and quality improvement and the second visit measured the extent of this progress and the College's capacity to improve. The focus of each review included observations of teaching and learning, discussion with learners and employers, scrutiny of student work and analysis of performance data.

The success of Highlands College's journey to self improvement is attributable to a number of factors, which provide valuable lessons to colleges seeking out a similar goal:

- **The sustained enthusiasm of the senior team and a relentless commitment to improvement:** through systematic arrangements focused on improvement.
- **A personal sense of accountability to the Island's community:** given the lack of learner choice on the Island and the close community, the College ensured that the provision was of the highest standard.
- **Long-term stability of the composition of the College management team:** managers identified with the College and felt that they were part of the College.
- **Complete honesty in the self-assessment process:** the absence of adverse consequences meant staff could be more honest and the constructive criticism provided by external critical friends created internal positive pressure for change.
- **Development of a sense of ownership in the improvement model:** the College's adaptation of an existing model engendered a sense of ownership by College staff and gave them the opportunity to demonstrate their commitment to quality improvement.
- **High levels of trust across the College:** managers were trusted to both engage with staff to formulate and implement QA arrangements, and to act on the outcomes.
- **The use of highly experienced, former senior inspectors as key external reviewers:** the presence of a College Inspector who managed the self improvement and built an in-depth knowledge of the context in which it operated contributing to its credibility.

Summary

Governance fulfils a key role in relation to the strategic management and leadership of a college, helping to shape the vision and mission of the institution as well as maintain quality and a secure financial footing. Although a number of models are currently in operation in England, the dominant approach ensures the interests of a wide range of stakeholders are reflected in a set of shared goals and objectives. However, the often large and unwieldy nature of some of these boards can undermine their effectiveness and limit the extent to which ideas and the strategic direction of the college are constructively challenged.

Moving forward in context of the skills strategy and localism agenda, colleges may need to develop governance structures that are capable of ensuring institutions remain *"first and foremost local organisations"*[347] serving the needs of local learners, while also meeting the demands of employers and fulfilling a wider role in the *"leadership of place"*.[348] Alternative structures are beginning to emerge; however, the sector-wide implementation of these approaches will require further changes to the legislative framework.

Effective governance goes hand in hand with effective leadership. New models based on the principles of collaboration, co-operation and facilitation are likely to be required if colleges are to realise the vision of the 'Big Society' and extend their reach beyond the provision of learning into their local communities. College principals along with their governing bodies may, therefore, need to prioritise community development[349] and ensure that *"the curriculum and wider institutional ethos reflect the principles of the Big Society, so that learners develop as citizens who embody the values and practices of the Big Society"*.[350] To achieve this, colleges could consider moving away from transactional approaches to leadership and embrace more transformational models which empower staff at all levels to play their part within a framework of distributed leadership. However, this also creates a number of challenges for the sector, including upskilling staff and college leaders and shifting organisational culture and attitudes.

The introduction of distributed models of leadership also has implications for the development of effective accountability structures. Within this framework, it will be as important to ensure accountability is extended horizontally and vertically *within* colleges as well as to key stakeholders, such as LEPs, local authorities, and employers, *outside* the institution. However, increasing local accountability also creates tensions for colleges when success in the eyes of community stakeholders does not reflect success as defined by funders and government.

---

347   Howard, U. (2009).
348   HayGroup (2010).
349, 350   LSIS (2010a).

8 Conclusions

This section summarises the key findings from the literature review. It identifies what we know based on the evidence as well as the areas where further research is needed to inform the continued and successful evolution of the FEC sector in England.

The literature review set out to explore the existing relationship between colleges and their communities in order to develop a better understanding of how they: contribute to local/community leadership (that is, as leaders of skills, as leaders in general and as trainers of leaders) ; shape and implement learning and skills policy; and define and deliver the adult curriculum. The purpose of the review was to help develop a vision for the sector in which colleges form the 'dynamic nucleus' of their local learning ecology, working in partnership with a range of public and private sector organisations from within and outside the education community.

The extensive review of UK and international literature revealed that colleges across the developed world are operating within a fast-moving policy environment. The evolution of FE systems is also shaped and influenced by local social, economic and political circumstances. As a result, there are discernable differences in emphasis and models of operation in different parts of the world and translating international practice into an English context presents some challenges.

Despite their differences, providers also have much in common. In particular, their commitment to providing opportunities for a wide range of learners, including those that missed out on education the first time around. There is a wealth of evidence to demonstrate that many colleges in England (and elsewhere) are deeply embedded in their communities and support learners to fulfil their potential both personally and professionally. Colleges achieve this in a number of ways. They work alone and in conjunction with others, including partnership organisations, employers, the voluntary and community sector, the wider public sector and learners themselves, to identify their specific needs as well as the needs of the local labour market.

Where possible, the priorities of these stakeholder groups are reflected in college strategic plans which in turn shape and inform the development and delivery of the curriculum. It is acknowledged that further work is required to ensure the views of non-traditional learners and those who are furthest from the education system are better represented.

The curriculum in English FECs is designed to equip learners with the skills they need to play an active role in the labour market as well as the attributes they need to engage fully in their communities and wider society; in this way colleges add public value to their communities by contributing to wider social and economic objectives. However, the extent to which colleges are able to effectively respond to the needs of their communities is constrained by a number of factors, including the lack of stability and a coherent long-term strategy for the sector.

The Coalition Government is implementing measures designed to reduce bureaucracy and simplify funding with a view to increasing the flexibility and responsiveness of colleges. Although it is early days, and the true extent and impact of these changes is not yet known, it is suggested that the new legislation may free colleges *from* some of the constraints that have previously inhibited them, but it stops short of providing colleges with the freedom *to* innovate and fully respond to the needs of locally defined priority groups.[351] In addition, fresh tensions have been created by the latest skills strategy that present the sector with a series of new challenges. These include reconciling: minimum contract levels with the drive to increase competition by encouraging new entrants into the market; minimum performance levels with widening participation objectives; the needs of communities with the new funding eligibility criteria; and the demands of employers with the needs of individuals. Colleges need even greater flexibility to shift funding across ages, geographical locations and types of learner in order to respond to their communities in the most effective and cost-efficient way. However, it is acknowledged that a system of this nature requires a considerable degree of trust on behalf of government and the funding agencies as well as a shift in account-

---

351 Hodgson, A. and Spours, K. (2009).

ability away from 'Big Government' towards local communities and stakeholders.

Existing approaches to governance and accountability are unlikely to be fit for purpose in this emerging context; new models based on collaboration, co-operation and facilitation that extend the role of college leaders into their communities and enable them to jointly define key success indicators with local stakeholders will be required. However, structural change of this nature also has implications for the leadership and management of colleges. Current approaches will also need to evolve in order to distribute responsibility for both the strategic and operational management of the organisation to a wider range of suitably qualified staff, freeing up senior managers to become more outward facing.

In the absence of Regional Development Agencies, there is a lack of clarity and consistency in local skills planning. Although LEPs are evolving to fill the void, they are yet to become fully established. Although it is widely acknowledged that colleges, as a lead provider of skills, have an important role to play in the LEP, the extent and nature of their involvement varies from region to region. Further research is required to establish the effectiveness of LEPs in shaping local skills policy as well as the models which most successfully engage key partners, including colleges, in this process.

Despite these constraints, there is also substantial evidence to demonstrate that colleges have a significant impact on the individuals they serve, in some cases having a transformational effect on them as individuals and their subsequent life chances. There is also evidence that colleges are impacting on employers through the provision of tailored programmes designed to address skills needs which are holding businesses back. However, the return on investment that employers who invest in training achieve is not fully understood; as the market for skills becomes increasingly competitive and employers are expected to shoulder more of the costs, further research to establish the financial and other business benefits of training will be required. Similarly, there is limited evidence on the social return on investment in skills. For example, the extent to which the benefits of learning to the individual extend to their communities has not been systematically examined and further research in this area is also required.

The literature review has revealed substantial evidence of the extent and nature of the relationship between colleges and their communities; however, it has also highlighted a number of important challenges for the future. As a 'dynamic nucleus' at the heart of their local communities, colleges will increasingly have to take account of, as well as respond to, the needs of a diverse range of stakeholders, including LEPs, Local Authorities, and employers, some of whom will have conflicting priorities. Collaboration and partnership will be central to this process; however, developing and maintaining successful partnerships represents a key challenge in itself. There is a plethora of research on effective partnership development as well as examples of good practice to draw upon. However, the prevailing culture of competition between providers will need to be reconciled if true partnership working is to become a reality.

Colleges serve a diverse range of learners and have an established track record of widening participation amongst those that are often under-represented in further and higher education. One of the principal ways in which they engage the most disadvantaged is through outreach activities. Numerous examples of successful outreach work are captured in the literature. However, outreach is costly both in terms of time and resources. This existing good practice could be under threat as budgets are cut. Information and communications technology could offer a partial solution, but further research is required to ensure it is applied in the appropriate way within adult learning. In addition, research has identified that more could be done to utilise college assets and resources for the wider benefit of their communities. An indirect benefit of this could be to expose potential learners from hard to reach groups to the college environment in a non-threatening way, which could in turn help to overcome some of their preconceived ideas about colleges and studying in further education. However, utilising college premises in this way generates a number of issues and further research is required to analyse the costs versus the benefits as well as resolve the practical and legal constraints.

In conclusion, there is much for which FECs should be proud. As a sector, they add considerable value to individuals, organisations and wider society through the provision of skills and the contribution they make to wider social and economic objectives. More could be gained if they were given the freedom and flexibility to extend their reach into communities and strengthen their community leadership. However, it is equally important to recognise that other organisations also add considerable value to their communities. The ultimate challenge is to develop a vision and framework for the future role of colleges in their communities that ensures each partner can play to their strengths.

Appendix 1 The causes of complexity in the skills system

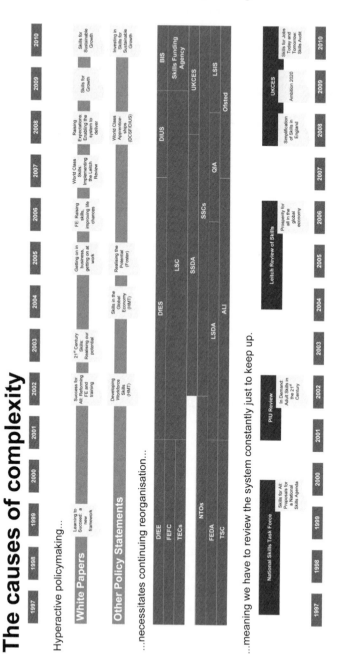

Figure 1: The causes of complexity in the skills system. [352]

---

352 Brown, D., Harris, M. and Fletcher, T. (2011).

Appendix 2 Typology of organisational learner-engagement

TYPES OF PARTICIPATION, ACTIVITIES AND TOOLS

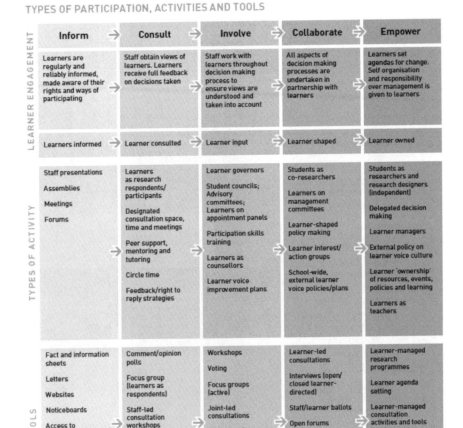

	Inform →	Consult →	Involve →	Collaborate →	Empower
LEARNER ENGAGEMENT	Learners are regularly and reliably informed, made aware of their rights and ways of participating →	Staff obtain views of learners. Learners receive full feedback on decisions taken →	Staff work with learners throughout decision making process to ensure views are understood and taken into account →	All aspects of decision making processes are undertaken in partnership with learners →	Learners set agendas for change. Self organisation and responsibility over management is given to learners
	Learners informed →	Learner consulted →	Learner input →	Learner shaped →	Learner owned
TYPES OF ACTIVITY	Staff presentations Assemblies Meetings Forums →	Learners as research respondents/participants Designated consultation space, time and meetings Peer support, mentoring and tutoring Circle time Feedback/right to reply strategies →	Learner governors Student councils; Advisory committees; Learners on appointment panels Participation skills training Learners as counsellors Learner voice improvement plans →	Students as co-researchers Learners on management committees Learner-shaped policy making Learner interest/action groups School-wide, external learner voice policies/plans →	Students as researchers and research designers (independent) Delegated decision making Learner managers External policy on learner voice culture Learner 'ownership' of resources, events, policies and learning Learners as teachers
TOOLS	Fact and information sheets Letters Websites Noticeboards Access to documents, minutes, plans etc →	Comment/opinion polls Focus group (learners as respondents) Staff-led consultation workshops Staff-led questionnaires, interviews etc (closed – staff-led) →	Workshops Voting Focus groups (active) Joint-led consultations Interviews (open – staff-directed) →	Learner-led consultations Interviews (open/closed learner-directed) Staff/learner ballots Open forums →	Learner-managed research programmes Learner agenda setting Learner-managed consultation activities and tools development

Figure 2: Typology of organisational learner engagement.[353]

---

353 Rudd, T., Colligan, F. and Naik, R. (2006).

Appendix 3 Roles and responsibilities of employer-led bodies in England

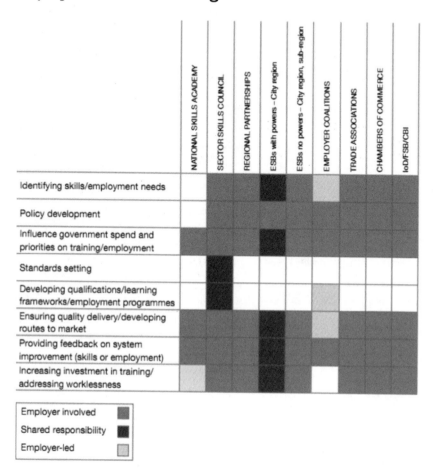

Figure 3: Roles and responsibilities of employer-led bodies in England.[354]

354 UKCES (2010).

Appendix 4 Types of employer engagement

The typology sets out a range of activity, under three broad headings:

1 Employers as *stakeholders,* in which they provide leadership through their involvement in the design, development, management, delivery and assessment of learning. Examples include:
   - providing work experience places
   - acting as visiting speakers
   - advising on the curriculum and its assessment
   - participating in college governance
2 Employers as *consumers*, in which they purchase diagnostic services and skills development from LSC-funded providers. Examples include:
   - purchasing training needs analysis services to identify workforce development needs
   - using information, advice and guidance services to source training provision
   - buying bespoke training for updating
   - using customised day release or regular provision as part of company training
3 Employers as strategic partners, in which there is sustained interaction between employers and the planners and providers of learning. Examples include:
   - using LSC sector providers as sources of support for business development
   - collaborating with planners in developing new provision for the benefit of their own company and the wider sector
   - contributing in cash or in kind to new or updated resources for learning – joint ventures and shared training facilities
   - sharing or subsidising specialist staff.

Table 1: Types of employer engagement.[355]

---

355 Macleod, D. and Hughes, M (2005).

PART THREE

REFERENCES AND BIBLIOGRAPHY

References and bibliography

157 Group (2009) *Getting the learning bug is the key to recovery*. London: 157 Group.

157 Group (2010a) *Leadership of locality: Leading the way in transforming standards in city schools*. London: 157 Group.

157 Group (2010b) *Strong Colleges Build Strong Communities*. London: 157 Group.

157 Group (2011a) *Adult further education – the unfinished revolution*. London: 157 Group.

157 Group (2011b) *Doing More for Less: An international dialogue about the challenges facing vocational and community colleges*. London: 157 Group.

157 Group and CfBT (2011) *Leading Learning in Further Education*. London: 157 Group.

Aked, J., Michaelson, J. and Steuer, N. (2010) *The role of local government in promoting well-being: Healthy communities programme*. London: Local Government Improvement and Development

Aldridge, F. and Tuckett, A. (2009) *Narrowing Participation: The NIACE Survey on Adult Participation in Learning*. Leicester: NIACE

Alexander, T. (2010) 'Learning to Be Powerful.' *Adults Learning*, 22 (2), pp.16-19.

Amalathas, E. (2010) *Learning to Learn in Further Education: A Literature Review of Effective Practice in England and Abroad*. Reading: CfBT Education Trust

Amey, M. J., Eddy, P. L. and Campbell, T. G. (2010) Crossing Boundaries Creating Community College Partnerships to Promote Educational Transitions. *Community College Review,* 37 (4), pp.333-347.

Andresén A., Kværndrup, S. and Glahn, N. (2010) *The Danish Folkehøjskole*. Copenhagen: The Royal Danish Ministry of Foreign Affairs.

AoC (2008) *My College, My Community: Further Education Colleges and Community Cohesion*. London: AoC.

AoC (2009a) *Economic Impact Studies*. [Online] Available from: www.aoc.co.uk/download.cfm?docid=D2647FD7-ABED-4EDA-BF8FECA5516C8D27 [Accessed 26/09/2011].

AoC (2009b) *Hiding the Wiring: Best Practice Guide for Communicating with Employers*. London: AoC.

AoC (2010) *College Key Facts: Summer 2010*. London: AoC.

AoC (2011a) *College Key Facts: Summer 2011*. London: AoC.

AoC (2011b) *Colleges in England at August 2011*. [Online] Available from: www.aoc.co.uk/en/research/college-key-facts.cfm [Accessed at 01/08/2011].

Arnott, S. (2011) 'Regional businesses call for clarity on LEPs plan.' *Independent*. 1st February 2011. [Online] Available from: www.independent.co.uk/news/business/news/regional-businesses-call-for-clarity-on-leps-plan-2200354.html [Accessed at 01/06/2011].

Aspden, J. and Birch, D. (2005) *New Localism – Citizen Engagement, Neighbourhoods and Public Services: Evidence from Local Government*. London: Local and Regional Government Research Unit, Office of the Deputy Prime Minister.

Atkinson, M. (2010) 'A glance into FE's collaborative future.' *FE Focus, Times Educational Supplement*, 8th January. [Online] Available from: www.tes.co.uk/article.aspx?storycode=6032816 [Accessed 08/06/2011].

Attwell, G. and Hughes, J. (2011) *Pedagogic Approaches to Using Technology for Learning Literature Review*. London: LLUK.

Australian Education Network (2011) *Australian Colleges*. [Online] Available from: www.australian-universities.com/colleges [Accessed at 16/08/2011].

Avis, J. (2009) 'Further education in England: The new localism, systems theory and governance.' *Journal of Education Policy* , 24 (5), pp.633-648.

Banks, C. N. (2010) *Independent Review of Fees and Co-funding in Further Education in England: Co-investment in the skills of the future*. London: BIS.

Barton, D., Appleby, Y., Hodge, R., Tusting, K. and Ivanic, R. (2006) *Relating Lives and Learning: Adults' Participation in a Variety of Settings*. London: National Research and Development Centre.

Beck, J. (2003) *Community focused schools: Draft framework document*. Cardiff: Cardiff Council Schools Service.

Becta (2008) *Harnessing Technology for Further Education, Skills and Regeneration A progress report*. Coventry: Becta.

Becta (2010a) *Harnessing Technology Review 2009: The role of technology in further education and skills*. Coventry: Becta.

Becta (2010b) *Sector Survey Further Education Colleges 2009-2010 Analytical Report*. Loughborough: Becta.

Becta. (2006) *ICT and e-Learning in Further Education: Management, Learning and Improvement*. Coventry: Becta.

Bennett, N., Wise, C., Woods, P. and Harvey, J. (2003) *Distributed Leadership*. Nottingham: National College for School Leadership.

Billett, S. and Seddon, T. (2004) 'Building community through social partnerships around vocational education and training.' *Journal of Vocational Education and Training*, 56 (1), pp.51-67.

Birch, E. R., Kenyon, P., Koshy, P. and Wills-Johnson, N. (2003) *Exploring the social and economic impacts of adult and community education*. Adelaide: National Centre for Vocational Education Research.

BIS (2010a) *Investing in Skills for Sustainable Growth*. London: BIS.

BIS (2010b) *Local growth moves up a gear as Business Minister announces growth package for local enterprise partnerships*. [Online] Available from: http://nds.coi.gov.uk/content/Detail.aspx?ReleaseID=419462&NewsAreaID=2 [Accessed 13/05/2011].

BIS (2010c) *Local Growth: Realising Every Place's Potential*. Norwich: TSO.

BIS (2010d) *New Challenges, New Chances: Next Steps in Implementing the Further Education Reform Programme*. London: BIS.

BIS (2010e) *Skills for Sustainable Growth*. London: BIS.

BIS (2011) *Colleges given more freedom to deliver skills for employment and growth*. 9th August 2011. [Online] Available from: http://nds.coi.gov.uk/content/Detail.aspx?ReleaseID=420758&NewsAreaID=2 [Accessed at 10/08/2011].

BIS and Skills Funding Agency (2010) *The Learning Revolution*. London: BIS.

Blanden, J, Draca, M. and McIntosh, S. (2005) *The Economic and Social Returns to FE Colleges*. London: DfES.

Blaug, R., Horner, L., Kenyon, A. and Lekhi, R. (2006) *Public Value and Local Communities A Literature Review*. London: The Work Foundation.

Bolton, T. (2011) *Sink or Swim? What Next for Local Enterprise Partnerships?* London: Centre for Cities.

Boyle, D., Coote, A., Sherwood, C. and Slay, J. (2010) *Right here, right now: Taking co-production into the mainstream*. London: NESTA.

Bradley, S., Johnes, J. and Little, A. (2010) Measurement and Determinants Of Efficiency And Productivity In The Further Education Sector In England.(Report). *Bulletin of Economic Research*, 62 (1), pp.1-30.

British Council (2007) The Netherlands Market Introduction. [Online] Available from: www.britishcouncil.org/eumd-information-background-netherlands [Accessed at 16/08/2011].

Brown (1985) and Turner (1991) Cited in: Gross, R. (1996) *Psychology: The Science of Mind and Behaviour*. London: Hodder and Stoughton. p. 489.

Brown, D., Harris, M. and Fletcher, T. (2011) *Reforming the skills system: Lessons learned the hard way*. Leicester: CFE and IOD.

Brown, D., Hughes, T. and Fletcher, T. (2010) *A top-down, bottom-up study of the UK employment and skills systems*. Leicester: CFE and UKCES.

Brown, J. (2008) *Social investment for community development: Completing the half-built house*. London: New Economics Foundation

Bynner, J. (2009) *Lifelong Learning and Crime: A Life-course Perspective: IFLL Public Value Paper 4*. Leicester: NIACE.

Cabinet Office (2010) *Building the Big Society*. [Online] Available from: www.cabinetoffice.gov.uk/sites/default/files/resources/building-big-society_0.pdf [Accessed at 18/07/2011].

Campbell, D. and Hongwei, Y. (2010) 2010 Community College Futures Assembly Focus: Effective Leadership-addressing the Graduation Challenge in the 21st Century, Community *College Journal of Research and Practice*, 34 (11), pp. 865-868.

Capey, M. (1999) *LEAs and Lifelong Learning. Slough: National Foundation for Educational Research*. London: LSIS.

Carpentieri, J. D. and Vorhaus, J (2010) The social value of further education and adult learning. In: Dolphin, T. and Clifton, J. (eds.) *Colleges 2020*. London: Institution for Public Policy Research, pp.34-46.

Carr-West, J. (2010) *People Places Power: How Localism And Strategic Planning Can Work Together*. London: Centre for Local Democracy at the LGiU.

Cartwright, P., Chapman, McGilp, J., Skilbeck, M., Toomey, R., de Souza, M., Gaff, J. and Williams, I. (2004) Lifelong learning, adult and community education in rural Victoria, Australia: A multi-agency approach to community building. *Development and Learning in Organizations*, 18 (5) pp.17-19.

CBI (2006) *Transforming Further Education – Further Skills for Success: Competition Delivers for Learners*. London: Confederation of British Industry.

CBI (2009) *Reaching Further: Workforce Development Through Employer-FE college Partnership*. London: CBI.

CEL (2007) *Further Education, Communities and Local Government – Exploiting the Potential, CEL*. Seminar briefing paper, 5th September 2007. Lancaster: CEL.

CEL and DIUS (2008) *Recruiting and Supporting Student Governors in Further Education and Sixth-form Colleges*. Lancaster: CEL.

Centre for Enterprise (2007) *Skills in Context*. Glasgow: Future Skills Scotland.

CFE (2008) *Skills Utilisation Literature Review*. Glasgow: Scottish Government Social Research.

CFE (2009a) *Beyond Known Unknowns: A Further Exploration of the Demand for Higher Level Skills from Businesses* Leicester: CFE.

CFE (2009b) *Identifying the Contribution of FE Providers to Local Priorities, Partners and Places*. Leicester: CFE and LSIS.

CFE (2010) *Offenders in Custody Apprenticeship Pilot Evaluation*. Coventry: LSC and CFE.

CFE (2011) *Research to assess preparation for and changes arising from the new FE reforms and skills policies*. London: BIS.

Chapman, R. (2006) *A Practical Guide to Employer Engagement*. Market Harborough: Association for College Management.

Chaves, C. (2006) Involvement, development, and retention: theoretical foundations and potential extensions for adult community college students.(Report). *Community College Review*, 34.(2), Winter 2006, pp.139.

CIPFA and Scotland's Colleges (2010) *Delivering Good Governance in Scotland's Colleges: A Framework (Consultation Draft)*. [Online] Available from: www.cipfa.org.uk/ scotland/download/final%20version%20for%20consultation%20clean.pdf [Accessed at 17/08/2011].

Clark, T. (2008) *OECD Thematic review of tertiary education. Update of Country Background report for United Kingdom*. Paris: OECD.

ColegauCymru (2011) *Modernising Education Structures Favoured by Colleges*. 28th June 2011. [Online] Available from www.collegeswales.ac.uk/en-GB/modernising_education_structures_favoured_by_colleges-249.aspx [Accessed at 16/08/2011].

Colleges Northern Ireland (2011) *Education*. [Online] Available from: www.anic.ac.uk/education.aspx [Accessed at 04/10/2011].

Collinson, D. (2007) Editorial Introduction. In: Collinson, D. (ed.) *Practitioner Research Projects - Volume 4: Leadership and the Learner Voice*. Lancaster: CEL. pp.4-11.

Collinson, D. (2010) *2006–2010 Overview of The CEL/LSIS Lancaster Leadership Research Programme: Summaries of 71 Practitioner Research Reports*. Coventry: LSIS.

Collinson, D. (ed.) (2007) *Practitioner Research Projects - Volume 5: Collaborative Leadership*. Lancaster: CEL.

Collinson, D. (ed.) (2008) *Practitioner Research Reports – Volume 8: Distributed and Shared Leadership*. Lancaster: CEL.

Collinson, D. and Collinson, M (2009) 'Blended leadership': Employee perspectives on effective leadership in the UK further education sector. *Leadership*, 5 (3), pp.365-380.

Collinson, M. and Collinson D. (2007) *Communities of leadership in FE: Lancaster University Management School Working Paper 2007/021*. Lancaster: Centre for Excellence in Leadership.

Collinson, M. and Collinson, D. (2005) *The Nature of Leadership: Communities of Leadership in FE*. Lancaster: CEL.

Collinson, M. and Collinson, D. (2007) *Faith in the Community: Leadership Challenges in the Learning and Skills Sector*. Lancaster: CEL.

Collinson, M. and Collinson, D. (2008) *Exploring Effective Employer Engagement and Learner Voice.* Lancaster: CEL.

Commission on Colleges in their Communities (2011) *A dynamic nucleus: Colleges at the heart of local communities.* Leicester: NIACE.

Commission on Integration and Cohesion (2007) *Our Shared Future.* Wetherby: Commission on Integration and Cohesion.

Corbyn, Z. (2011) They've Started, but will they finish. *Times Higher Education,* 3rd march 2011, pp 39-41.

Cormier, D. (2008) Rhizomatic education: community as curriculum. *Innovate,* 4 (1998).

Corney, M. (2007) *Still Waiting for Big Ideas on Adult Skills.* Reading: CfBT Education Trust.

Currie, A. and Brown, D. (2009) *Training Quality Standard: One year on evaluation summary.* [Online] Available from: www.trainingqualitystandard.co.uk/uploaded/files/TQS-evaluation-summary-2009.pdf [Accessed 09/09/11].

Davis, P. (2011) *The role of local enterprise partnerships in tackling skills needs.* London: 157 Group.

Dean, A. (2010) *The implications of the Comprehensive Spending Review on: Employment, Further Education, Higher Education and the Voluntary and Community Sector.* Exeter: Marchmont Observatory, University of Exeter.

deCastro, B. S. and Karp, M. M. (2008) *A typology of community college-based partnership activities.* New York: Community College Research Center.

Department for Communities and Local Government (2008) *Guidance for Local Authorities on How to Mainstream Community Cohesion into Other Services.* London: Department for Communities and Local Government.

Department for Communities and Local Government (2009) *Strong and prosperous communities – The Local Government White Paper.* London: Department for Communities and Local Government.

Department for Communities and Local Government (2010a) *Local Growth: Realising Every Place's Potential.* London: DCLG.

Department for Communities and Local Government (2010b) *Localism Bill.* London: Department for Communities and Local Government.

Department for Employment and Learning (2008) *Guide for Governors of Further Education Colleges.* [Online] Available from: www.delni.gov.uk/guide_for_governors_fe_colleges_-_11_sept.pdf [Accessed 04/10/2011].

Department for Employment and Learning (2011) *Background to the further education sector.* [Online] Available from: www.delni.gov.uk/index/further-and-higher-education/further-education/fe.htm [Accessed at 04/10/2011].

Department for Employment and Learning (2011) *Review of Further Education - FE Means Business.* [Online] Available from: www.delni.gov.uk/index/further-and-higher-education/further-education/femerger.htm [Accessed 04/10/2011].

Department of Education, Science and Training (2007) *OECD Thematic review of tertiary education. Country Background report for Australia.* Paris: OECD.

DfES (2006) *Further Education: Raising Skills Improving Life Chances.* Norwich: HMSO.

Diaz, V. (2010) 'Web 2.0 and emerging technologies in online learning.' *New directions for community colleges,* 150, Summer 2010, pp.57-66.

DIUS (2008) *Informal Adult Learning – Shaping the Way Ahead: Consultation Response Analysis Report.* London: DIUS.

DIUS (2008) *Raising Skills, Improving Life Chances: Giving Learners and Employers a Say: Guidance for Further Education Institutions on Consultation.* London: DIUS.

DIUS and AoC (2008) *The Role of Further Education Providers in Promoting Community Cohesion, Fostering Shared Values and Preventing Violent Extremism Consultation Document.* London: DIUS.

DIUS, AoC, ALP, and NIACE (2008) *FE Works: Supporting Individuals, Employers and Communities.* London: DIUS.

Doherty, K. J. (2009) 'English further education through American eyes.' *Higher Education Quarterly*, 63 (4), pp.343-355.

Dougherty, K. J. (2010) 'US community colleges and lessons for British further education colleges.' In: Dolphin, T. and Clifton, J. (eds.) *Colleges 2020.* London: Institution for Public Policy Research. pp.93-105.

Drakenberg, M. (2001) 'The Professional Development of Teachers in Sweden.' *European Journal of Teacher Education,* 24 (2) pp.195-204.

Drodge, S. (2000) 'Partnership as a theme in the management of external influences on further education colleges.' *Education Through Partnership*, November 20004, 2, p.52-59.

Dunavin, C. (2010) 'The Power of Partnerships = The Power of Success!!!' *Community College Journal of Research and Practice*, 34 (11), pp.878-882.

Edwards, C. and Wynch, J. (1993) 'American community colleges: a model for British further education?' *Educational Management and Administration*, 21 (1,), pp 19-25.

EMSI (2008) 'The Economic Contribution of City College Norwich.' In: AoC (2009) *Economic Impact Studies.* [Online] Available from: www.aoc.co.uk/download.cfm?docid=D2647FD7-ABED-4EDA-BF8FECA5516C8D27 [Accessed 26/09/2011].

EMSI (2008) The Economic Contribution of Huddersfield Technical College. In: AoC (2009) *Economic Impact Studies.* [Online] Available from: www.aoc.co.uk/download.cfm?docid=D2647FD7-ABED-4EDA-BF8FECA5516C8D27 [Accessed 26/09/2011].

Erlt, H. and Statsz, C. (2010) 'Employing an 'Employer-led' Design? An Evaluation of the Development of Diplomas.' *Journal of Education and Work*, 23 (4), pp.201-317.

Evans, K. (1996) 'Reshaping colleges for the community in Canada and Britain.' *Research in Post-Compulsory Education*, 1 (2), pp.199-218.

Evans, L. (2005) *Educating adults – transforming communities*, paper presented at the 35th Annual SCUTREA Conference, 5-7 July 2005, University of Sussex. Bangor: University of Bangor.

Farrelly, D. (2005) 'Building bridges: Armagh College's lifelong learning initiative.' *Adults Learning*, 16 (8), pp.20-21.

Feinstein, L. (2002) *Quantitative Estimates of the Social Benefits of Learning, 1: Crime.* London: Centre for Research on the Wider Benefits of Learning.

Feinstein, L., Budge, D., Vorhaus, J. and Duckworth, K. (2008) *The Social and Personal Benefits of Learning: A Summary of Key Research Findings.* London: Centre for Research on the Wider Benefits of Learning.

Feinstein, L., Duckworth, K. and Sabates, R. (2004) *A Model of the Intergenerational Transmission of Educational Success*. London: Centre for the Research on the Wider Benefits of Learning.

Feinstein, L., Galindo-Rueda, F. and Vignoles, A. (2004) 'The labour market impact of adult education and training.' *The Scottish Journal of Political Economy*, 51 (2), pp.266–280.

Fielding, M. (2004) 'Transformative approaches to student voice: theoretical underpinnings, recalcitrant realities.' *British Educational Research Journal*, 30 (2), pp.295-311.

Fielding, M. (2006) 'Leadership, radical student engagement and the necessity of person-centred education.' *International Journal of Leadership in Education*, 9 (4), pp.299-313.

Fletcher, M.(ed.) (2000) *For Better or Worse: The Influence of FE Franchising on Learning*. London: Further Education Development Agency.

Forde, C. (2000) 'The college in the community: Location as a means of combating educational inequality.' *The Irish Journal of Education*, 31, pp.63-77.

Forrest, C., Lawton, J., Adams, A., Louth, T. and Swain, I. (2007) 'The Impact of Learner Voice on Quality Improvement.' In: Collinson, D. (ed.) *Practitioner Research Projects - Volume 4: Leadership and the Learner Voice*. Lancaster: CEL. pp. 13-29.

Foster, A (2005) *Realising the potential: A review of the future role of further education colleges*. Nottingham: DfES Publications.

Freire, P. (1996) *Pedagogy of the Oppressed*. London: Penguin.

Frumkin, L., Koutsoubou, M. and Vorausm, J. (2008). *Minority Ethnic Groups: Success Rates in Further Education – A Literature Review*, QIA (LSIS). Cited in Howard, U. (2009) *FE Colleges in a New Culture of Adult and Lifelong Learning: IFLL Sector Paper 7*. Leicester: NIACE.

Fryer, R. H. (2008) *Lifelong Learning, Citizenship and 'Belonging': A briefing paper*. Liverpool: Liverpool University.

Fulbright Center (2011) *Overview of the Dutch Secondary Education System*. [Online] Available from: www.fulbright.nl/cache/f4/f4c740ce8378ea8480232907ccb1840d/31.Overview SecondEducation.pdf [Accessed at 16/08/2011].

Fulton-Calkins, P. and Milling, C. (2005) 'Community-College Leadership – an Art to be Practiced: 2010 and Beyond.' *Community College Journal of Research and Practice*, 29, pp.233-250.

Gallacher, J., Mayes, T. and Crossan, B. (2007) *Understanding and Enhancing Learning Cultures in Community-Based Further Education*. Glasgow: Centre for Research in Lifelong Learning.

Garlick, S., Davies, G., Polèse, M. and Kitagawa, F. (2006) *Supporting the Contribution of Higher Education Institutions to Regional Development. Peer Review Report*. Paris: OECD.

Gates, P., Brown, E., Clegg, C. and Din, S. (2008) *Leadership in Adult Community Education: Political Decisions and the Development of Social Capital*. Lancaster: CEL.

Gibney, J. and Murie, A. (eds.) (2008) *Toward a 'New' Strategic Leadership of Place for the Knowledge-based Economy*. Leeds: Academy for Sustainable Communities.

Gibney, J., Copeland, C. and Murie, A. (2009) 'Toward a 'New' Strategic Leadership of Place for the Knowledge-based Economy.' *Leadership*, 5 (1), pp.5-23.

Gibney, J., Yapp, C., Trickett, L. and Collinge, C. (2009) *The 'New' Place-Shaping: The Implications for Leaders in the Further Education Sector.* London: LSIS.

Gleeson, D., Abbott, I. and Hill, R. (2009) *Creative Governance in Further Education: the art of the possible?* London: LSIS.

Goozee, G. (2001) *The development of TAFE in Australia.* Adelaide: National Centre for Vocational Education Research.

Great Britain Parliament (2009) *Apprenticeships, Skills, Children and Learning Act 2009.* London: HMSO.

Green, A., Preston, J. and Sabates, R. (2003) *Education Equality and Social Cohesion: A Distributional Model.* London: Centre for Research on the Wider Benefits of Learning.

Grubb, W. N. (2003) *The Roles of Tertiary Colleges and Institutes: Trade-offs in Restructuring Postsecondary Education.* Paris: OECD.

Hammond, C. and Feinstein, L. (2005) 'The effects of adult learning on self-efficacy.' *London Review of Education*, 3 (3), pp.265-87.

Hammond, C. and Feinstein, L. (2006) *Are Those Who Flourished at School Healthier Adults? What Role for Adult Education? WBL Research Report 17.* London: Centre for Research on the Wider Benefits of Learning.

Hannon, P., Pahl, K., Bird, V., Taylor, C. and Birch, C. (2003) *Community-focused provision in adult literacy, numeracy and language: an exploratory study.* London: National Research and Development Centre for Adult Literacy and Numeracy.

Hardy, B. (2010) 'Why is there a lack of central funding for enterprise education at further education colleges?' *Research in Post-Compulsory Education*, 5 (3), pp. 301-316.

Hawley, J. (2006) *Public Private Partnerships in Vocational Education and Training: International Examples and Models.* [Online] Available from: http://siteresources.worldbank.org/EXTECAREGTOPEDUCATION/Resources/444607-1192636551820/Public_Private_Partnerships_in_Vocational_Education_and_Training.pdf. [Accessed at 05/10/2011].

Hayes, J. (2011) *Vision for Further Education*, speech presented at Warwickshire College, Rugby 15th June 2011. [Online] Available from: www.bis.gov.uk/news/speeches/john-hayes-vision-for-further-education [Accessed 18/07/2011].

HayGroup (2010) *FE Colleges: new challenges and new opportunities.* London: HayGroup.

Hillage, J., Uden, T., Aldridge, F. and Eccles, J. (2000) *Adult Learning in England: A Review.* Brighton and Leicester: IES and NIACE.

Hippach-Schneider, U., Krause, M. and Woll, C. (2007) *Vocational Education and training in Germany: Short description.* Luxembourg: Cedfop.

HM Government (2010) *Local Growth: Realising Every Place's Potential.* London: TSO.

Hodgson, A. and Spours, K. (2009) *Collaborative Local Learning Ecologies: Reflections on the Governance of Lifelong Learning in England. IFLL Sector*

Paper 6. Leicester: NIACE

Hooley, T. and Watts, A. G. (2011) *Careers Work with Young People: Collapse or Transition?* Derby: International Centre for Guidance Studies.

House of Commons Business, Innovation and Skills Committee (2010) *The New Local Enterprise Partnerships: An Initial Assessment: First Report of Session 2010-11, Volume 1.* London: HMSO.

Howard, U. (2009) *FE Colleges in a New Culture of Adult and Lifelong Learning: IFLL Sector Paper 7.* Leicester: NIACE.

Howell, C. (2008) *Thematic Analysis: Space. Learning Landscape Project.* Cambridge: University of Cambridge.

Hubert, P., Sallis, E. and Jones, G. (2009) Developing Self Regulation at Highlands College. In: Collinson, D. (ed.) *Practitioner Research Reports – Volume 12: Researching Self-Regulation in FE Colleges.* London: LSIS, pp.27-44.

Hubert, P., Sallis, E. and Pearce, J. (2010) *Work Based Learning: The Leadership Challenges for College and businesses.* Coventry: LSIS.

Huisman, J. (2003) *Higher education in Germany – Country report.* Enschede: Centre for Higher Education Policy Studies

Humphreys, R. (2001) *An independent review of the governance arrangement of further education institutions in Wales.* Cardiff: Department for Children, Education, Lifelong Learning and Skills.

Hyland, T. and Merrill, B. (2003) *The changing face of further education: lifelong learning, inclusion and community values in further education.* London: Routledge Falmer.

Institute for Public Policy Research & PricewaterhouseCoopers (2009) *Towards a Smarter State.* London: Institute for Public Policy Research.

Institute for Public Policy Research & PricewaterhouseCoopers. (2010) *Capable communities: Public sector reform: the next chapter.* London: Institute for Public Policy Research.

IOE (2010) *Organisation and governance in post-compulsory education: where now for the Coalition Government?* Conference notes from: A London Region Post-14 Network Conference, October 2010, Institute of Education, University of London. London: IOE.

Jackson, K. (1995) Popular education and the state: a new look at the community debate. In Mayo, M. and Thompson, J. (eds.) *Adult Learning, Critical Intelligence and Social Change.* Leicester: NIACE, pp. 182-203.

James, D. (2011) Policy into practice: provider perspectives. In: Hodgson, A., Spours, K. and Waring, M. (eds.) *Post-compulsory Education and Lifelong Learning Across the UK: Policy, Organisation and Governance.* London: Institute of Education, University of London. Chapter 6.

James, S. (1998) (ed.) *FE: aspects of economic development.* London: FEDA

Jenkins, R. (2004) *Social Identity.* London: Routledge

Jessop, B (1998) The rise of governance and the risks of failure: the case of economic development. *International Social Science Journal,* 50 (155), pp.29-45.

JM Consulting (2009) *Costing Partnerships – collaborative arrangements between HEIs and FECs.* London: HEFCE.

Katsifli, D. and Green, K. (2010) *Making the Most of the Student Voice in Further Education.* London: 157 group and Blackboard.

Kelly, S. (2007a) *Employer Engagement in the Further Education Sector.*

Lancaster: CEL.

Kelly, S. (2007b) *Innovative Approaches to Employer Engagement in Further Education*. Lancaster: CEL.

Kidner, C. (2011) *Scotland's Colleges*. Scottish Parliament Information Centre [Online] Available from:
www.scottish.parliament.uk/business/research/briefings-11/SB11-55.pdf [Accessed at 17/08/2011].

King, M., Widdowson, J. and Brown, R. (2008) *Higher education and colleges: a comparison between England and the USA*. London: CIHE.

Kisker, C. B. and Carducci, R. (2003) 'UCLA Community College Review: community college partnerships with the private sector - organizational contexts and models for successful collaboration.' *Community college review*, 31 (3), pp.55-74.

Kisker, K.B. (2007) Creating and sustaining community college-university transfer partnerships. *Community college review*, 34 (4), pp.282-301.

KPMG (2010) *Delivering Value for Money through Infrastructural Change*. Coventry: LSC.

Learning by Volunteering (2011) [Online] Available from:
http://learningbyvolunteering.org/ [Accessed at 18/07/2011].

Leitch, S. (2006) *Prosperity for all in the global economy – world class skills*. Norwich: HMSO.

Leney, T., May, T., Hayward, G. and Wilde, S. (2007) *International Comparisons in Further Education*. Nottingham: DfES Publications.

Levin, B. (2000) Putting Students at the Centre in Education Reform. *Journal of Educational Change*, 1 (2), pp.155-172.

Local Government Association (LGA)/157 Group/ British Chambers of Commerce (2010) *Local Learning and Skills Conversations: New Responses to Local Needs*. London: LGA.

LGA (2011) *Local learning and Skills Conversations: New Responses to Local Needs*. London: LGA.

Lord, P., Martin, K., Atkinson, M. and Mitchell, H. (2009) *Narrowing the gap in outcomes: what is the relationship between leadership and governance?* (LGA Research Report). Slough: NFER.

LSIS (2009a) *Community Cohesion and Social Exclusion – ESOL Learner's Perspective: Leadership Challenges*. Coventry: LSIS.

LSIS (2009b) *Leading the Learner Voice 2009: Dissemination of effective practice*. Coventry: LSIS.

LSIS (2010a) *Citizen Engagement*. Coventry: LSIS.

LSIS (2010b) *Northampton College: Learner voice and technology*. 16th September 2010. [Online] Available at:
www.excellencegateway.org.uk/page.aspx?o=298753 [Accessed 27/09/11].

LSIS (2010c) *The importance of being local: Reframing the role of learning and skills in the strategic development of place*. Coventry: LSIS.

LSIS (2010d) *The involvement of colleges in the Total Place pilots*. Coventry: LSIS.

LSIS and UKCES (2011) *Shaping the Community Scorecard Action Research Project: Final Report*. Coventry: LSIS.

LSN (2009) *For the sake of argument: Discussion and debating skills in citizenship*. London: LSN.

LSN (2009) *Listening to Learners? Citizenship and Learner Voice*. London: LSN.

LSN (2010) *Engaging Employers to Drive up Skills: The Realities of Effective Employer Engagement – Current Opportunities and Challenges.* London: LSN.

Lundahl, L. (2002) From Centralisation to Decentralisation: governance of education in Sweden. *European Educational Research Journal,* 1 (4), pp.625-636.

Macleod, D. and Hughes, M (2005) *What we know about working with employers: a synthesis of LSDA work on employer engagement.* London: LSDA.

Mager, C. (2007) *Public Value and Leadership: Exploring the Implications.* Lancaster: CEL.

Matrix Knowledge Group (2009) *Lifelong Learning and Well-being: An Analysis of the Relationship Between Adult Learning and Subjective Well-being: IFLL Public Value Paper 3.* Leicester: NIACE.

Mauger, S. (2009) *Technological change: IFLL Thematic Paper 2.* Leicester: NIACE.

Mayo, M. (2000) Learning for active citizenship: Training for and learning from participation in area regeneration. *Studies in the Education of Adults* , 32 (1), pp.22-35.

McCrone, T., Southcott, C. and Evans, K. (2009) *Collaborative Good Practice Between Local Authorities and the Further Education Sector.* LGA Research Report. Slough: NFER

McGivney, V. (1999) *Informal Learning in the Community: A Trigger for Change and Development.* Leicester: NIACE.

McGivney, V. (2000) *Recovering Outreach: Concepts, Issues and Practices.* Leicester: NIACE.

McNair, S. (2009) *Migration, Communities and Lifelong Learning: IFLL Thematic Paper 3.* Leicester: NIACE

Merrill, B. (2000) *The FE college and its communities.* London: FEDA.

Merrill, B. and Hyland, T. (2001) Community, partnership and social inclusion in further education. *Journal of Further and Higher Education,* 25 (3), pp.337-348.

Merrill, B. and Hyland, T. (2003) *The Changing Face of Further Education: Lifelong Learning, Inclusion and Community Values in Further education.* London: Routledge /Falmer.

Meyer, S. (2006) 'Developing Learning Communities.' *Adults Learning,* 16 (6), pp.20-21.

Morgan, W. J. (2008) 'Social capital, citizenship and continuing education: What are the connections?' *International Journal of Continuing Education and Lifelong Learning,* 1 (1), pp 35-45.

Munro, N. (2009) 'Generous Dose of Dutch Courage.' *Times Education Supplement,* 6th November 2009. [Online] Available from: www.tes.co.uk/article.aspx?storycode=6027075 [Accessed at 16/08/2011].

National Assembly for Wales (2009) *Learning and Skills (Wales) Measure (2009).* [Online] Available from: www.assemblywales.org/bus-home/bus-legislation/bus-leg-measures/business-legislation-measures-ls.htm [Accessed at 16/08/2011].

NCC Group, HHES and Nottingham Trent University (2009) *ICT in FE & Skills, Impact Study.* Coventry: Becta.

NIACE (2005a) *Eight in Ten: Adult Learners in Further Education.* Leicester:

NIACE.

NIACE (2005b) *A NIACE response to the 10 key questions from Sir Andrew Foster's review of the future role of FE colleges.* [Online] Available from: http://archive.niace.org.uk/Organisation/advocacy/DfES/Foster-Review.htm [Accessed at [18/07/2011].

NIACE (2009) *Harnessing Technology Survey 2008/2009: Adult and Community Learning.* Coventry: Becta.

NIACE (2011) *Policy Briefing: The Wolf Report – Its Potential Impact on Adult Learning.* Leicester: NIACE.

Northampton College (2010) *New ways to give learners a voice.* 15ᵗʰ November 2010. [Online] Available at: www.northamptoncollege.ac.uk/news/item.aspx?NewsItem=678 [Accessed at 27/09/2011].

Northern Ireland Assembly (2011) *Committee for Employment and Learning Official Report (Hansard) – Briefing from Colleges Northern Ireland on Current Issues in Further Education.* 29ᵗʰ June. [Online] Available from: www.niassembly.gov.uk/record/committees2011/EmploymentLearning/110629 _CollegesNI.htm [Accessed at 04/10/2011].

Nuissl, E. and Pehl, K. (2004) *Portrait Continuing Education Germany.* 3rd ed. Bielefeld: W. Bertelsmann Verlag.

Office for National Statistics (2011) *Statistical Bulletin: Labour market statistics July 2011.* [Online] Available from: www.ons.gov.uk/ons/rel/lms/labour-market-statistics/lms-july-2011/labour-market-statistics.pdf [Accessed at 04/10//2011].

Office for the Deputy Prime Minister (2006) *Promoting Effective Citizenship and Community Empowerment. A guide for local authorities on enhancing capacity for public participation.* London: Office for the Deputy Prime Minister.

Ofsted (2004a) *The Responsiveness of Colleges to the Needs of Employers.* Manchester: Ofsted.

Ofsted (2004b) *Why Colleges fail.* Manchester: Ofsted.

Ofsted (2004c) *Why Colleges Succeed.* Manchester: Ofsted.

Ofsted (2008) *The role of adult learning in community renewal: Neighbourhood Learning in Deprived Communities programmes.* Manchester: Ofsted.

Ofsted (2009) *Identifying good practice: a survey of college provision in information and communication technology.* Manchester: Ofsted.

Ofsted (2010) *Learning together: How education providers promote social responsibility and community cohesion.* Manchester: Ofsted.

Palmer, D. (2009) 'Colleges may be the heart of communities but further education cannot be locally organised in a global economy.' *Guardian,* 24ᵗʰ February. [Online] Available from: www.guardian.co.uk/thetraininggame/comment-local [Accessed at 01/08/2011].

Peeke, G. (2003) 'Leadership in Further Education.' In: Brundrett, M., Burton, N. And Smith, R. (eds.) *Leadership in Education.* London: SAGE publications. pp.164-179.

Policy Governance (2011) *Policy Governance.* [Online] Available from: www.carvergovernance.com [Accessed at 18/07/2011].

Policy Research Institute (2007) *Role of Colleges in Community Cohesion: Rapid*

Review of Evidence. Coventry: LSC.

Preston, J. and Hammond, C. (2002)*The Wider Benefits of Further Education: Practitioner Views*. London: The Centre for Research on The Wider Benefits of Learning.

Putman, R. (2000) *Bowling Alone: The Collapse and Revival of American Community*. New York: Simon and Schuster

Putnam, R. (2004) *Education, Diversity, Social Cohesion and "Social Capital"*. Paris: OECD.

RSA/LSIS (2011) *The Further Education and Skills Sector in 2020: A Social Productivity Approach*. London: RSA/LSIS.

Rudd, T., Colligan, F. and Naik, R. (2006) *Learner Voice: a handbook from Futurelab*. Bristol: Futurelab.

Rutter, J. (2010) The global college. In: Dolphin, T. and Clifton, J. (eds.) *Colleges 2020*. London: Institution for Public Policy Research, pp.47-64.

Saunders, D. M., Brosnan, K., Walker, M., Lines, A., Storan, J. and Acland T (eds.) (2004) *Learning transformations: changing learners, organisations and communities* London: FACE.

Sawbridge, S. J. (2000) *Leadership for achievement in further education: a review of the literature*. FEDA.

Sawbridge, S. J. (2001) 'Leadership in further education: A summary report from a review of the literature.' In: Horsfall, C. (ed.) *Leadership issues: raising achievement*. London: LSDA. pp.5-18.

Schofield A., Matthews, J. and Shaw, S. (2009) *A Review of Governance and Strategic Leadership in English Further Education: The future challenges facing governance and strategic leadership in FE*. Coventry: LSIS.

Schuller, T. (2009) *Crime and Lifelong Learning. IFLL Thematic Paper 5*. Leicester: NIACE..

Schuller, T. and Watson, D. (2009) *Learning Through Life: Inquiry into the Future for Lifelong Learning*. Leicester: NIACE.

Schwab, K. (ed.) (2010) *The Global Competitiveness Report 2010-2011*. Geneva: World Economic Forum.

Schwinn, C. and Schwinn, D. (2000) 'A Call to Community: The Community College Role in Comprehensive Community Development.' *Community College Journal*, 70 (5), pp.24-30.

Shury, J. (2010) *National Employer Skills Survey for England 2009: Main Report, Evidence Report 23*. London: UKCES.

Shuttle, J. (2007) 'Learner Involvement in Decision Making.' In: Collinson, D. (ed.) *Practitioner Research Projects – Volume 4: Leadership and the Learner Voice*. Lancaster: CEL. pp.30-48.

Simon, J. (1998) *FE: Aspects of Economic Development*. London: FEDA.

Skills Funding Agency (2010) *Further Education: New Horizon – Investing Skills for Sustainable Growth*. London: Crown Copyright.

Skills Funding Agency (2011) *Qualifications Credit Framework: Frequently Asked Questions. Updated: July 2011*. [Online] Available from: http://readingroom.lsc.gov.uk/SFA/QCF_-_July_2011_FAQs.pdf [Accessed at 01/08/2011].

Slack, K and Thomas, L. (2003) 'Developing an evaluation framework: assessing the contribution of community-based and work-based approaches to lifelong learning amongst educationally marginalised adults.' *Research in Post-*

Compulsory Education, 8 (1), pp.19-38.

Smith, C., Gidney, M., Barclay, N. and Rosenfeld, R. (2002) 'Dominant logics of strategy in Further Education Colleges.' *Research in Post-Compulsory Education*, 7 (1), pp.45-62.

Smyth, J. (2006) 'Educational leadership that fosters student voice.' *International Journal of Leadership in Education*, 9 (4), pp.279-284.

Spours, K., Coffield, F. and Gregson, M. (2007) 'Mediation, translation and local ecologies: understanding the impact of policy levers on FE colleges.' *Journal of Vocational Education and Training*, 59 (2), pp.193-211.

Spours, K., Hodgson, A., Brewer, J., and Barker, P. (2009) 'Improving progression for younger learners in further education colleges in England.' *Journal of Vocational Education & Training* , 61 (4), pp.431-446.

Spratt, S., Simms, A., Neitzert, E. and Ryan-Collins, J. (2009) *The Great Transition: A tale of how it turned out right*. London: New Economics Foundation

Stein, D.S. (2002) 'Creating Local Knowledge through Learning in Community: A Case Study.' *New Directions for Adult and Continuing Education*, Fall 2002, 95, pp.27-40.

Swedish National Agency for Higher Education (2006) OECD *Thematic review of tertiary education. Country Background report for Sweden*. Paris: OECD.

Taylor, S. (2003) *Learning and Skills for Neighbourhood Renewal: Summary Report on Research for the Neighbourhood Renewal Unit*. London: LSDA.

TES (2011) *Colleges win right to award foundation degrees*. [Online] Available from: www.tes.co.uk/article.aspx?storycode=6107489 [Accessed 12/08/2011].

Tett, L., Crowther, J. and O'Hara, P. (2003) Collaborative partnerships in community education. *Journal of Education Policy*, 18 (1), pp.37-51.

The Aspen Institute (2011) *Skills for America's Future*. [Online] Available from: www.aspeninstitute.org/policy-work/economic-opportunities/skills-for-americas-future [Accessed at 18/07/2011].

The IEA College of TAFE (2011) *About the IEA College of TAFE*. [Online] Available from: www.iea.ac.pg/schools/tafe/tafe_frameset.html [Accessed at 16/08/2011].

The Poverty Site (2011) *Working-age adults without qualifications*. [Online] Available from: www.poverty.org.uk/59/index.shtml [Accessed at 01/08/2011].

The Scottish Government (2011a) *Colleges*. [Online] Available from: www.scotland.gov.uk/Topics/Education/UniversitiesColleges/17135 [Accessed at 17/08/2011].

The Scottish Government (2011b) *Curriculum, Assessment & Qualifications*. [Online] Available from: www.scotland.gov.uk/Topics/Education/Schools/curriculum [Accessed at 17/08/2011].

Training Quality Standard (2011) *Training Quality Standard*. [Online] Avialable from: www.trainingqualitystandard.co.uk/index-2.html [Accessed at 15/04/2011].

Tuckett, A. (2005) *The Untidy Curriculum: adult learners in further education*. Leicester: NIACE.

U.S. Department of Education (2009) *Partnerships between community colleges and prisons providing workforce education and training to reduce recidivism*.

Washington: U.S. Dept of Education.

UCU (2010) *Student participation in quality assurance in the FE and HE sectors.* London: UCU.

UCU (2010) *The Impact of Student Satisfaction Surveys on Staff in HE and FE Institutions.* [Online] Available from: www.ucu.org.uk/media/pdf/8/d/ucubrief_studentsatissurveys_oct10.pdf [Accessed at 25/03/2011].

Uden, T. (2003) *Education and training for offenders.* Leicester: NIACE.

UKCES (2010) *What's The Deal? The Employer Voice in the Employment and Skills System.* London: UKCES.

UKCES (2011) *Review of Employment and Skills.* London: UKCES.

UNESCO-UNEVOC (1998) *Cooperation with the World of Work in Technical and Vocational Education. A: The Policy Level – Studies from Hungary, Romania and Sweden. B: The Institution Level – A Study from the Russian Federation.* Berlin: UNESCO.

Vocademix (2011) *The Independent College Partnership: Colleges of Further Education Going Mutual.* [Online] Available from: www.vocademix.com/downloads/The%20Independent%20College.pdf [Accessed 01/07/2011].

Volunteering England and LSC (2008) *Assessing the impact of volunteering on the further education sector.* London: Volunteering England.

Walker, P. and Whitehead, S. (2011) *Connected Conversations: Tackling big issues by linking small conversations.* London: New Economics Foundation.

Wallace, S. and Gravells, J. (2010) Telling a compelling story: managing inclusion in colleges of further education. *Management in Education*, 24 (3), pp.102-106.

Ward, J. (2009) 'What Did Lifelong Learning Networks Ever Do for Us?' *Adults Learning*, 21 (1), pp.30-31.

Warren, J. (2000) 'Collaboration between a small rural community college and a large industrial corporation for customized training.' *Community College Journal of Research and Practice*, 24 (8), pp.667-679.

Waters, S. and Moran, A. (2001) 'Working partnership links different worlds.' *Adults Learning*, 13 (4), pp.17-20.

Westwood, A. and Jones, A. (2003) *FEUK: Productivity, Social Inclusion and Public Sector Reform.* London: The Work Foundation.

Widdowson, J. (2010) 'Colleges in their local context.' In: Dolphin, T. and Clifton, J. (eds.) *Colleges 2020.* London: Institution for Public Policy Research. pp.88-92.

Wikipedia (2011a) *Economy of Sweden.* [Online] Available from: http://en.wikipedia.org/wiki/Economy_of_Sweden [Accessed at 16/08/2011].

Wikipedia (2011b) *Education in Scotland.* [Online] Available from: http://en.wikipedia.org/wiki/Education_in_Scotland [Accessed at 17/08/2011].

Wikipedia (2011c) *Further Education.* [Online] Available from: http://en.wikipedia.org/wiki/Further_education [Accessed at 17/08/2011].

Wikipedia (2011d) *German Model – Vocational Training.* [Online] Available from: http://en.wikipedia.org/wiki/German_model#Vocational_training [Accessed at 16/08/2011].

Wolf, A. (2008) Adult learning in the workplace: creating formal provision with impact. *Teaching and Learning Research Briefing*, 59.

Wolf, A. (2009). *An adult approach to further education*. London: Institute of Economic Affairs.

Wolf, A. (2011) *Review of Vocational Education – The Wolf Report*. Cheshire: DFE.

Wong, L. T. and Toraskar, H. B. (2009) A review of community college education in Hong Kong and India. *International Journal of Continuing Education and Lifelong Learning*, 1 (2), pp. 69-81.